Praise for *We Set the Night on Fire*

"Martha Shelley's *We Set the Night on Fire* is a memoir of one woman's revolt against all that sought to contain her. Martha moves through responses to tyranny that defined the twentieth century, beginning with her parents' and grandparents' flight from antisemitism, followed by her own struggle against the Gay persecution that was a defining feature of the mid-twentieth-century United States political and social contract. Martha reminds us of how seemingly casual hatred harms our lives, and of the enormous effort and solidarity across race, gender, and sexualities necessary to expose and challenge that hatred.

"Her story could be the story of many, brought up in the United States by undocumented parents doing all they could so their children would not experience the hunger and oppression that had scarred their lives. Martha continued this tradition of courage when she stepped forward after Stonewall to become one of the Lesbian/Gay/Trans/Queer people who founded the Gay Liberation Front and began a global movement for justice."
—**Flavia Rando**, coordinator of the Lesbian Herstory Archives and director of its Lesbian Studies Institute

"Meeting the brash, funny, smart, caring Martha Shelley years ago helped push me out of the closet into the human world. Now, thanks to this engaging memoir, you too can meet this inspiring justice activist. Bravo, Martha!"
—**Jonathan Ned Katz**, author of *The Daring Life and Dangerous Times of Eve Adams*

"Martha Shelley has written a book of heart-turning directness that is both politically and sexually astute. Her writing has simplicity, honesty, and beauty—and is also at times funny as hell. *We Set the Night on Fire* is that perfect rare place where politics and art unite, as it traces her journey from lesbian feminist discovery to the revelation that even fellow revolutionaries, after the passion and intimacies of battle, *can* knife you in the back. Shelley has never abandoned her Brooklyn Jewish roots, but

instead has flowered with them, intellectually and morally. For anyone looking to change and deepen his or her life, this is a must-read."
—**Perry Brass**, Gay Liberation Front, author of *The Lover of My Soul* and *King of Angels*

"Martha Shelley, lesbian founder of the Gay Liberation Front, documents her gay coming of age in *We Set the Night on Fire*. It is a slow burn through Shelley's activist awakening as a young woman via the civil rights, anti–Vietnam War, and Second Wave lesbian feminism before arriving at ground zero—the Stonewall Riots in New York City."
—**Cassandra Langer**, author of *Romaine Brooks: A Life*

"Martha Shelley is a true pioneer and hasn't stopped exploring. *We Set the Night on Fire* is a road map and a way to use the knowledge of yesterday to be prepared for tomorrow."
—**August Bernadicou**, president of the LGBTQ History Project

WE SET THE NIGHT ON FIRE

Igniting the Gay Revolution

MARTHA SHELLEY

CHICAGO
REVIEW
PRESS

Published by Chicago Review Press Incorporated
814 North Franklin Street
Chicago, Illinois 60610
ISBN 978-1-64160-941-8

Library of Congress Control Number: 2023930229

Typesetting: Nord Compo
Unless otherwise indicated, all images are from the author's collection

Printed in the United States of America
5 4 3 2 1

For my wife Sylvia Allen
la migliore artigiana
who helped me every step of the way

and for all the younger warriors
because in every generation
a new pharaoh arises to enslave us
and in every generation
we must renew the fight for freedom

CONTENTS

INTRODUCTION

THIS IS THE STORY OF MY DEVELOPMENT as an activist in the women's and gay liberation movements of the 1960s and '70s. Looking back on those years from my current age of seventy-nine, I know that I've had a very lucky life.

I believe that ninety-five percent of life is luck.

It was my good fortune that my grandparents and parents had the gumption to leave Eastern Europe well before the Holocaust, which meant that I was born in safety, in New York City. I was healthy. Though I caught most of the childhood diseases that they didn't have vaccines for, I missed getting polio, and the others left no long-term effects. I was also intelligent. That and robust health I owe to good genes and the good nutrition my mother provided, for which I deserve no credit.

The economy flourished during those years. Though our family never rose to middle-class status, City College was free, and we kids received an excellent education.

The civil rights and anti–Vietnam War movements inspired me, and inspired the Second Wave of the women's movement. New York City was a center of feminist ferment, and I was lucky to be living there, to meet and work with others like me—and even more, lucky to be at ground zero during the Stonewall Riots.

The other five percent—the decisions we make—is what shapes our lives. A high IQ is nice, but what really directs your destiny is a good heart, or the lack thereof. You can be the top student in your class, like Joseph Goebbels, then spend your life writing propaganda for the Nazi Party. Or you can put that five percent over which you do have control to the lifelong task of seeking justice. My hope is that this book inspires an army of younger activists to do just that.

PROLOGUE

June 28, 1969

I'm taking two women from Boston on a tour of Greenwich Village. I'm a member of the New York chapter of the lesbian organization Daughters of Bilitis, and the visitors want to start a chapter in their city. It's a hot Saturday night. The sky is clear, the moon just about full. We're walking along Christopher Street in Greenwich Village when we encounter a group of young men throwing things at cops.

The Bostonians are taken aback and seem frightened. "What's that?" one asks.

"Ah, it's just a riot," I reply, thinking the guys were protesting the Vietnam War. "We have them all the time."

I forget about the incident until Monday morning, when I finally get to read the New York Times *report: ". . . police raided a bar . . . well known for its homosexual clientele. . . . The young men threw bricks, bottles, garbage, a few pennies, and a parking meter at the policemen . . . the Stonewall Inn, 53 Christopher Street . . ."*

I'd never heard of the Stonewall Inn before, but I'm on fire, inspired by the civil rights movement, and by the antiwar and women's movement demonstrations that I'd actually participated in. Now it's our time to rise up. Gay people's time. I immediately phone Jean Powers, president of the NY DOB chapter. "We gotta have a protest march."

Jean works in computers and is in the closet. She hesitates. I know she won't be marching out in public. But then she tells me to talk to the Mattachine Society, the local gay men's organization. "If they agree, we can jointly sponsor it."

The march I called for and helped organize took place one month later, on July 27. Yet I didn't start out in life wanting to become a gay activist, or an activist of any kind.

1

A SMALL ACT OF REBELLION

The Peak of Empire

I spent my childhood in the best of all possible cities, in the best nation that ever was. At one time I was sure that other countries would soon realize this, adopt our language and customs, and unite under our government. Parents, teachers, radio broadcasts, and the newspapers my father brought home extolled America's magnificence. Rebellion wasn't merely absurd; it was unthinkable.

Our family rented a one-bedroom apartment in the Crown Heights neighborhood of Brooklyn, New York. My parents had the bedroom. After I graduated from the crib, I slept in a junior bed in their room. When my sister came along, she got the crib and then the junior bed, and I was moved to the living room couch. Mom scrubbed a few small items in the kitchen sink but took most of the wash to the Laundromat. On clear days she'd bring it home wet and hang it out the kitchen window on clotheslines that stretched across the courtyard between our apartment building and the next one. Those lines crisscrossed the entire yard, ground floor to third floor.

Some mornings we'd hear singing in the courtyard. Then the mothers would wrap a coin or two in bits of newspaper and throw them to

Me and my kid sister, Jeannette,
on our block in Brooklyn.

the singers, who were always Black and mostly women. After a shouted thank you, the singers would pick up the coins and move on to the next building. I didn't understand the words of the songs and thought they were opera, since I didn't understand opera either when it was broadcast on the radio, and I thought the performers were respected professionals. All those coins seemed like wealth to my four-year-old self.

We had an ice box, not a fridge, and the iceman would deliver a big block every morning. We didn't get a TV until a year or so after the neighbors bought theirs. At one point we got a phone—a party line, shared between four families. If you picked up the receiver and heard someone talking, you hung up and tried again later.

But most important in my memory, we went to the country every summer. Dad managed to buy a used car and fixed it up himself. My parents rented a bungalow, and right after Memorial Day they packed the car.

Mom, my sister Jeannette, my cousin Ira, and I spent the entire summer in the Catskills, returning home after Labor Day. Dad would drive up for weekends and his two-week vacation. For three months we swam, picked berries, breathed fresh air, and ate farm-fresh food—all on a single income. Even a middle-class family today can't begin to afford anything like this.

We were at the peak of empire but didn't realize it. After WWII, ordinary American workers—at least the White ones—were better off economically than they had ever been. Dad had a civil service job, which was a vast step up for him from the insecurity of the Depression years. Mom had known hunger as a child in Poland and as an immigrant in Cuba, but now she could put three meals on the table.

In our apartment in Brooklyn, Dad left for work, usually before I got up, and came home at five o'clock. I remember watching him count out his pay, seventy dollars per week take-home, of which he kept five dollars for subway fare—a nickel a ride—and incidentals. He handed the rest to Mom, to pay the rent and buy what we needed.

A Christmas party at the Navy Regional Accounts Office where my father worked. I got to shake hands with the admiral.

When I was a bit older, my father commented that, according to government statistics, we were always just on the line between poor and middle class but never managed to get a leg up. I thought our family was doing just fine. We had the necessities—three meals, a roof overhead—and what I considered the most important luxuries: a stash of comic books, chocolate pudding for dessert on Friday, and lox and bagels on Sunday morning.

An Odd Child

I knew I was different. When we kids played house, I was either the father or the brother. When we played pirate ship, I was the captain, my cousin Ira was the first mate, and my younger sister was the princess we captured and held for ransom. In third grade, after lunch, the teacher would pass out paper and crayons. The boys would all draw tanks launching artillery shells, fighter planes shooting flaming bullets, and other engines of war. The girls drew stereotypical brides: a half circle for the face, three elongated ovals for the hair (one on top and two on the sides), a heart shape for the upper part of the décolleté gown, and a bell shape for the lower part. Pointy-toed shoes peeked out from under the bell. I drew cactuses in the desert, or octopuses and fish under the sea.

I read a lot. In fourth grade, I got my first pair of glasses. In elementary school I was always at the top of the class, but in 1950, intelligence did not correlate with popularity. Mostly I was let alone, but sometimes other kids called me "egghead" or "four-eyes" and opined that I had swallowed the dictionary.

My parents, on the other hand, encouraged my interest in science. They took me to the Bronx Zoo once or twice a year, and to the Museum of Natural History and Hayden Planetarium. At the planetarium I got to see the sky show, step on a scale that told me what I'd weigh on Jupiter, and climb onto the enormous Willamette meteorite.

My ambition was to be the first little girl on Mars. I imagined stepping out of a spaceship and onto the surface of the red planet, greeting the little green natives. In my mind's eye I would look very much as I did then: around four feet tall, bespectacled, and wearing a knee-length wool jumper, my hair caught in two brown braids. I didn't envision a space suit. Despite practically memorizing some children's books on astronomy, I still hadn't absorbed the fact that Mars has very little atmosphere and an average surface temperature of minus eighty degrees Fahrenheit.

Jeannette was three years younger, more sociable, and more popular. I don't remember what her childhood interests were, but she did like pretty clothes and resented the hand-me-downs we got from older cousins. She had fair skin and blonde straight hair over a high forehead like our maternal grandmother's. My complexion was olive, my hair dark and curly, my forehead shorter—I looked like my mother. Mom would say that I was the smart one while Jeannette was the pretty one, unintentionally wounding both of us. Jeannette had plenty of intelligence and eventually became a successful attorney. But Mom had internalized a blonde, WASP standard of beauty, and in that respect I fell short, as she did herself.

A Small Act of Rebellion

In addition to being bright, I was a good child. I dutifully recited the Pledge of Allegiance each morning, then sat with folded hands taking in the biblical passage our principal, Miss Dalrymple, read over the public address system. She picked verses intended to inspire virtue—various psalms, the Ten Commandments, the Sermon on the Mount, 1 Corinthians 13—omitting the bits about sex, war, and stoning sinners. She also avoided any mention of Jesus, which might have offended our parents; the Crown Heights neighborhood was largely Jewish in those days. In any case, I am grateful to Miss Dalrymple for the psalms, which were my first exposure to poetry.

At the same time that I was earnestly working to be a good patriotic little girl, I also kept hearing hints that America might not be such an earthly paradise after all. There were the whispers of frightened grown-ups, and news articles I didn't have the background to comprehend.

The summer I was eight, I picked berries in the Catskills with an elderly neighbor, a refugee from somewhere in Eastern Europe. She kept muttering, "Subwoisive, subwoisive. Whatever you do, they call you subwoisive." I may not have understood the meaning of the word *subversive*, yet the incident stayed with me. Joseph McCarthy and the House Un-American Activities Committee were riding high that year, persecuting anybody they could accuse, however falsely, of being a Communist.

The Red Scare was in full swing, and earlier that year the Supreme Court had ruled that teachers could be required to sign legally binding loyalty oaths. If you didn't sign, you would lose your job. The teachers' union and the ACLU opposed the law, as it infringed on freedom of speech and of association—not to mention violating common sense. As the *New York Times* wrote, a "really dangerous Communist would of course neither admit his affiliation nor hesitate to take the oath."

The summer I was nine, I read an excruciatingly detailed description of the electrocution of the Rosenbergs, who had been convicted of spying for the Soviet Union. I had a gut feeling—still do—that the Rosenbergs must have been picked out especially because they were Jewish. I was sickened by it, horrified, just as I was by accounts of the Holocaust, thinking that whoever wrote the article did so with a kind of sadistic pleasure. Recently I found and reread that same *New York Daily News* article. It was even more vicious than my memory. The Jewish establishment, terrified of being associated with Communism, even joined in calling for their deaths.

And then, at age eleven, I entered junior high school and began to rebel. I was sitting in homeroom when the teacher passed out little slips of paper for us all to sign. It seems that some kids had been bringing water guns to school and squirting each other in the lunchroom or the yard. The little slips said that we understood it was forbidden to bring water guns onto school property. Once we had signed, they could use it as justification for expelling us if we violated the rule.

I was an honors student and didn't even own a water pistol at the time. *This is exactly like a loyalty oath*, I thought, and refused to sign.

My teacher brought me down to the principal's office. Two school officials took turns badgering me. They'd call my parents. They'd suspend me from class. I argued that I had never carried such a dangerous weapon onto the premises and didn't intend to. They kept me for what seemed like an hour, beating me down until I did sign.

As an adult I came to understand that those teachers and officials had learned their lesson very well. They'd all had to swear the hated oath in order to keep their jobs, and now they were using the same kind of coercion to make me sign a similarly idiotic declaration.

Mine was a small act of rebellion, and unsuccessful. But I came away believing that I was right and despising the teachers who'd bullied me. In that respect it *was* a victory, because they hadn't brainwashed me into accepting their point of view.

2

ORIGINS

I'VE BEEN SORTING THROUGH THE CONTENTS of an old shoebox in one of my desk drawers—a few old photos, passports, certificates, and mementos like my mother's darning egg and my father's drafting tools. They stir up memories of tales passed down through the generations.

My Mother's Story

My mother, Gitl Dina Bojankosky, was born in 1914 in Nowy Dwor, a town twenty-four miles from Warsaw. I couldn't find the census figures for that year, but in 1921 there were seventy-eight hundred total residents, of which half were Jewish.

Mom had nothing good to say about her childhood in Poland. Her earliest memory was of an incident that took place one cold winter when she was a toddler. Grandma Leah had just given birth to a second child. Grandpa Samuel, who worked with his brother Ben in the kosher meat business, was out of town when the pogrom began. Leah snatched up Gitl and the baby, ran into the woods, and hid all night in the snow. By morning the violence had ended—and her newborn had frozen to death. Later, when Gitl was old enough to attend school, gentile kids threw stones at her and called her "Christ killer." A murderer in the area went free because the only witnesses in the case were Jews, and since they couldn't swear on the New Testament, their word was not acceptable in court.

Even in good times, my family—and most of the other residents of
the Jewish shtetl—weren't well off. Great-Uncle Ben said that he had
two wooden spoons, one for meat dishes and one for dairy; to tell them
apart, a nail had been driven through the handle of the dairy spoon.
"Every time I ate with it, it scratched me."

Then came World War I. Much of the heavy fighting between Russia
and Germany took place in Poland. Ben said that at one time he and
another business partner lay trapped in the underbrush for two days
while opposing armies fired at each other over their heads. Farmers
all over Poland didn't dare go out in the fields to plant or harvest for
fear of being caught in the crossfire. Retreating units looted what they
could and burned the rest, leaving parts of the country uninhabitable.
The result was widespread hunger.

When the war ended, the victorious allies set up a soup kitchen in
Nowy Dwor. Leah felt ashamed to beg, so she sent four-year-old Gitl
out with a bucket, to stand in line. But other neighbors—also Jewish;
meanness knows no ethnic boundaries—advised the soldiers not to give
her any. "Her family is rich," they said. It seems that my grandfather
had found some colored tiles and cemented them to the common wood-
stove that served both for cooking and heating in every home. To the
neighbors this attempt at beautification marked the family as wealthy.
Gitl had to go home with an empty bucket. "The soup had meat in it,"
she said sadly, forty years later. "I can smell it to this day."

Grandpa Samuel managed to get his family out of Poland in 1921.
They intended to go to New York, but in that same year, the United
States passed an act limiting the number of immigrants from certain
countries, mainly those from Southern and Eastern Europe. My grandparents and their three children went to Cuba instead. (A fourth child
was born in Havana.) There they were poor, but not persecuted. The
children were given Spanish names along with their Hebrew ones. Gitl
became Carmen.

Samuel found work in a button factory under conditions so harsh
that he still had nightmares about it in his eighties. As soon as the
children finished elementary school, they too were sent to the factories.
Food was expensive, and Leah knew next to nothing about nutrition.

Once, when Gitl/Carmen was sick, Leah took her to the doctor. "Give her vegetables," he said. "What are they?" she asked, and when he listed a few, she asked how to cook them. Despite the poverty, my mother had some good memories of those years. She learned the cha-cha, merengue, and rumba, and as a teenager attended socials at both the Jewish and Communist centers. "I just loved to dance. I didn't care about the politics," she assured me.

That assurance, coming shortly after the McCarthy era, was no doubt intended to protect me but failed to convince. This was the mother who taught me never to cross a picket line, the mother who joined the Workmen's Circle, with its pro-labor and pro-socialist agenda. If she did sympathize with the Communist Party, though, she ultimately became disillusioned. One of the boys she danced with in Havana was, as she put it, "an idealist. He went to Russia to help with the revolution and was murdered by Stalin" during one of the dictator's anti-Semitic purges.

During the 1920s Cuba became a favorite playground for robber barons like the Biltmores, corrupt politicians like New York City mayor Jimmy Walker, and so-called bohemians. They came for gambling, horse racing, golfing, country-clubbing, and the local prostitutes. Young Carmen saw only rich American tourists and thought that everyone in the United States was wealthy. She very much wanted to go to the "goldene medina," the golden land, but was still too young.

By the end of the decade the family had become citizens. I have Grandpa's naturalization certificate in that shoebox in my desk drawer. Dated November 19, 1928, it bears the signature of the Cuban president, Gerardo Machado.

Machado had started out as a popular leader but became increasingly dictatorial. When the Great Depression brought the island's sugar-based economy to its knees, people all across the political spectrum—from Communists to conservative veterans—began to revolt. Machado responded by having his secret police murder political opponents. Conditions in Cuba were even worse than in the United States.

In 1930, sixteen-year-old Carmen boarded a small boat, along with her younger brother Irving and perhaps a couple dozen other desperate immigrants, and crossed the open ocean to Florida. Even before facing the physical dangers of the journey, she would have had to come up with sufficient funds to pay smugglers and purchase false papers to present to any US officials who might have stopped and questioned her. From Miami she made her way to New York City, where she found work sewing in a garment factory. That first winter was terrible, as she wasn't used to the climate and couldn't afford a warm coat. But she did get another new name—Gussie.

Josefa, my mother's baby sister, admired Mom for undertaking such a perilous venture. "I didn't have the courage," Josefa said. Instead of leaving Havana and seeking her fortune elsewhere, she married a man in the jewelry trade, and they eventually came to New York. Later, when Mom married Dad and they had to struggle financially, Josefa lived in luxury. Unfortunately, Uncle Benito was a domestic tyrant, abusive to his wife and children.

Grandpa Samuel came on another boat. Once in New York he joined a local synagogue, where a member turned him in for the bounty money and he was deported. Discouraged, or perhaps unable to obtain funds to pay the smugglers, he didn't try again. Carmen and her brother were lucky—nobody betrayed them, and they stayed in New York.

Back in Havana, by 1933, the unrest had grown almost to the point of all-out war, and powers in the United States were worried. At President Roosevelt's behest, the US ambassador intervened in the conflict, arranging for Machado to go into what must have been a comfortable exile in Florida—and bringing in a regime controlled by Fulgencio Batista, who later turned out to be every bit as nasty as his predecessor.

Not long after Batista's government was installed, Grandpa Samuel had to go to a state office for some paperwork related to his citizenship. The bureaucrats said they couldn't find any of his records. Samuel made several trips before realizing that what they wanted was a bribe. Once he showed up with the necessary cash, the documents reappeared.

Much later, when Castro took over (in 1959, when I was fifteen), my mother said she supported him. "I'm not a Communist," she assured me once again, "but now every Cuban child will get medical care and have enough to eat."

My Father's Story

My father, Jacob Joseph Altman, was born in Brooklyn in 1912. His family moved to the United States before the change in immigration laws that prevented my mother from coming here.

Jacob's father, Reuben, was from Kishinev (Chişinău), an Eastern European city that was founded in 1436 as a monastic village. It became part of the Russian empire early in the nineteenth century. Reuben was born in 1889. According to the Russian census of 1897, when he was eight, the population had grown to 108,483, of which 50,237, or 46 percent, were Jewish. I only recently learned a little of that early history, since to Jews, the name Kishinev has become synonymous with the horrific pogroms of 1903 and 1905. Grandpa Reuben wouldn't tell me about life in the old country—"Don't ask!" he said gruffly—but my father filled me in.

As a teenager, Grandpa Reuben survived one of those pogroms by swimming across the river on the western edge of the city. At age twenty, on a visit to Odessa, he met a young woman named Yacha Weissbrot. He was tall and blond; Yacha was half a head shorter and plump, with long black braids. Yacha's mother, Rachel, was a widow. According to family legend, Rachel had a nice house with a large mirror in the front hall, which led Reuben to think her family was wealthy and spurred him to propose to Yacha. Later he discovered that there was no money, but, to give him credit, he stayed with her.

Soon after returning to Kishinev, he was drafted. In those days, each district was supposed to provide a certain number of its young men to the tsar's army for a six-year term, plus nine years in the reserves. The conscript might be shipped anywhere and might not see his family again for many years. Military rations were scant and certainly not kosher. Besides being taught his soldierly duties, he could expect to be beaten by the noncoms, who would also extort or simply steal from their subordinates. If he were Jewish, he'd likely be subject to additional abuse.

What Reuben did instead was emigrate. He arrived at Ellis Island in 1910, found work in the Garment District, and sent for his fiancée. To enter the country, you needed both marketable skills and family to look after you so you wouldn't become a public charge. Yacha declared that she was a seamstress and was going to live with an uncle. She took an American name, Jennie.

In 1911 Estelle, their first child, was born. In 1912 the twins, Jacob and David, came into the world, and Yacha/Jennie sent for her mother, who arrived shortly thereafter. Another girl, Charlotte, came along in 1915. The growing family lived in a small Brooklyn apartment, pulling out dresser drawers to use as cribs for the new babies.

Great-Grandma Rachel died in the 1918 flu pandemic. They laid her body in a coffin across two chairs in the living room—who could afford a funeral home? Little Jacob was devastated. His grandma had spent more time caring for the twins than their mother did.

Jennie was pregnant again but didn't want to bear another child during the pandemic and without her own mother's help. Birth control devices and information about them were illegal in those days. Seven-year-old Estelle watched as her mother tried to induce a miscarriage by climbing onto the cabinet of her Singer sewing machine and jumping down, repeatedly—to no effect. (Aunt Estelle told me that story when she herself was a grandmother.) That child was Benjamin. In 1922 their last child, Roslyn, was born.

Jennie never received a formal education and was illiterate, but she did her best to cope. She learned to write her name in English and to read and write numbers. Years later, when she was babysitting me, she demonstrated this skill with evident pride. She also showed me how she phoned her six grown children: an asterisk next to a group of seven numerals in her notebook meant she could dial those numbers and reach Estelle, a spiral meant Charlotte, and so on.

The family spoke Yiddish at home. Jacob, my father, didn't learn English until entering elementary school. The childhood memories he shared with me were of boyish mischief, much more cheerful than my mother's: running under the bellies of horses in the stables next door, while avoiding being kicked; stealing the raisins out of the challah bread Jennie had baked and left on the windowsill to cool, leaving only crumbs.

Jacob wanted to go to high school after completing the required eight grades, but Grandpa Reuben considered high school an unaffordable luxury. His children had to go to work as soon as they legally could. Jacob's first job, in 1926, was as a delivery boy for a local market. I don't know what other positions he held over the next three years, but once the Great Depression hit, he took whatever he could get—assistant in a doctor's office, assistant to an auto mechanic, office boy. At night he went to the local gym, trying to build enough muscle to lift garbage cans for the sanitation department—a civil service position!

One of the firms he worked for went out of business and couldn't pay his last week's wages. Instead, they gave him boxes of printed envelopes with penny stamps on them. That night Jennie stayed up late and steamed the stamps off, to sell to neighbors.

Uncle Dave—my father's twin—told me that Jacob had been a flaming radical during the Depression. Dad never said anything about that, not to me. His only political advice was to vote Democratic, because the Democrats let a few coins trickle down to the workers while the Republicans kept everything for themselves.

In 1938 Uncle Dave began to court Eva, a neighborhood girl who lived with her widowed mother. Grandpa Reuben told him to just have an affair with her, since she had no money. Dave replied, "I can't do that! She's a religious girl." Dave had a job digging ditches, but when the foreman called him a dirty Jew, he threw his shovel down and walked off. Grandpa was outraged. "You quit a *job*? Over *that*? Get out of my house—I'm not supporting you." Dave went to Eva's house and slept on the living room couch for a few days. Then he said, "We can't go on like this. Let's get married." And so they did. They lived to celebrate their sixtieth wedding anniversary.

In my observation, some respond to hardship by becoming harder, others by becoming compassionate. Grandpa Reuben was a tightwad and, according to my father, a "domestic tyrant." But on one occasion he showed affection to Cousin Larry by giving the boy a quarter. "Don't tell your grandmother," he whispered. That same day, Grandma Jennie handed Larry another quarter and instructed him not to tell Grandpa.

In later years, when an uncle captured family members on very short home movies—really minute-long clips—Grandpa leaned over and planted a kiss on his wife's cheek. This unusual display provoked gasps of surprise and laughter from the rest of the family.

By contrast, both my parents were generous and kind. They fought at times but never failed to help their children, or any relatives in need, and always expressed concern for the sufferings of others. Whatever virtues I possess I owe to them.

———————————

One evening soon after their marriage, Dave and Eva went out on a double date with Jacob and a new acquaintance named Gussie. "I couldn't tell the twins apart," Mom said. "So I waited. When Dave took Eva's hand, I knew who I was with."

My parents married in 1939. In order for my mother to obtain citizenship, Dad had to send her back to Cuba and sponsor her as an immigrant.

The young couple struggled financially, as did most Americans. The Depression wasn't over, but the official unemployment rate had decreased from 24.9 percent to 17.2 percent. (The real unemployment rate? Who knows?) The drought that had turned the Great Plains into a dust bowl had ended. No sooner had those black clouds settled than others arose, this time over Europe: that same year, Nazi Germany invaded Czechoslovakia, and then Poland.

At War and at Work

After the United States entered the war, Jacob was called up, but he was able to obtain deferments at various times because of myopia, his marital status, and Gussie's pregnancies. His experience as an auto mechanic's assistant proved useful: the government put him to work manufacturing ammunition. His drafting compasses and treasured micrometer are in the shoebox, too. When Gussie became pregnant, she stopped working in the garment industry and sat in front of the local movie palace selling war bonds.

By 1944 the official unemployment rate had dropped to 1.2 percent. The conventional wisdom is that the war lifted the country out of the Depression. Economist Robert Higgs disputes this, and I agree with him. "During the war the government pulled the equivalent of 22 percent of the prewar labor force into the armed forces," he writes. Bingo! Put unemployed people to work as soldiers, and your unemployment rate goes down.

However, these new soldiers found that military "jobs" were distinctly worse than civilian employment. The pay was scant, the food was wretched, and you couldn't quit or join a union and go on strike. Working conditions often resulted in death, maiming, or lifelong psychological damage.

Conditions at home weren't rosy, either, during the war. Most of the new civilian jobs that became available were in manufacturing. In that sector the workweek increased from 38.1 hours in 1940 to 45.2 hours in 1944, and the rate of disabling injuries per hour increased 30 percent.

During the war many basic consumer goods, including meat, butter, cooking oil, coal, and firewood, were rationed. You had to stand in long lines for them or pay a stiff premium on the black market. Some products, such as automobiles and nylon stockings, weren't produced at all. You could purchase a used car at elevated prices, but the tires and gasoline would be rationed.

My shoebox also contains some of the ration booklets, each with a few pages of unused stamps, tiny and fragile. Some say "coffee" or "sugar," or depict fruit or a stalk of wheat. Others have patriotic pictures: an aircraft carrier, a tank, a howitzer, Lady Liberty's torch. The name and address of the person each booklet was issued to is written on the cover: the baby (me), my father, my mother, Grandpa Samuel, and my mother's youngest sister, Pesa (her Spanish name was Josefa). Why Grandpa Samuel? It seems that my mother's parents came to the United States in 1943, while Mom was pregnant with me, and stayed for six months. Mom was able to sponsor them for permanent admission in 1947.

Oddly, the addresses on these booklets are the same, that of the apartment in Brooklyn where my family lived. During the war years, housing was scarce. The population was increasing by 1.1 percent per year (as compared to .68 percent during the Depression), but no one was building or even repairing the existing housing stock. Were all of us crammed into that one-bedroom apartment? I don't know.

In November 1947 Grandpa Samuel became a member of the Jewish Wurst Makers Benevolent Society. I have his union booklets—again, in the shoebox—showing that Samuel joined in November 1947 and paid dues every month until February 1954. One of them is printed in Yiddish and English, and opens with a statement of principles: "We, Jewish Wurst Makers, are an oppressed class, and we were more so oppressed by the bosses than any other worker in the same trade. We therefore decided to unite. . . ." After he'd retired, Mom told me that one of the union officers absconded with the pension funds that Grandpa Samuel and all his union brothers had paid into.

Samuel also became a member of an AFL affiliate, Amalgamated Meat Cutters and Butcher Workmen of North America. I have the dues booklets for this union dated from 1951 to 1966. Samuel would have been sixty-six when he joined and was still paying when he was eighty-one. I have no idea why. He certainly wasn't working in a sausage factory at that age.

3

SNAKES IN THE GRASS

As a child I was pretty well behaved. But during summer vacation, when we moved to the Catskills to escape New York's scorching streets, I managed to find trouble. I caught snakes, experimented on an unfortunate frog, hexed an older girl, and led a younger one astray.

Two Months in the Country

Starting when I was in elementary school, my parents would rent a place for the summer. Toward the end of May they'd drive over a hundred miles north to the Catskill Mountains, visit a few bungalow colonies, and pick one from among those within our price range and within a short walk from a swimming hole.

School let out at the end of May. Right after dinner on that last day and late into the night, Mom packed boxes of dishes, flatware, cooking utensils, clothing, and linens. We had to supply all these ourselves. Early the next morning she and Dad packed the old sedan. Boxes went in the trunk—so many of them that its lid wouldn't close and had to be tied down with clothesline. Pillows were stacked on the back seats, and Jeannette and Cousin Ira sat on them. Dad drove, with Mom beside him and me next to her. I had the front window seat, partly because I was the oldest and partly because I was the one who always got carsick.

In those days it took five to six hours to reach our destination. Halfway through, about fifty-two miles from Brooklyn, we stopped for lunch at the Red Apple Rest, a cafeteria-style eatery patronized by thousands of families heading to their summer rentals. I always ordered a hot dog. Half an hour later Dad would have to pull over so I could throw up.

We arrived at our bungalow late in the afternoon. At each colony it was pretty much the same: stove, refrigerator, table, and chairs in the kitchen; in the bedroom, iron bed frames with box springs and mattresses. Mom and Dad hauled in the boxes, put the kitchenware in the cabinets, and put sheets on the beds.

On Sunday evening Dad went home. For the rest of the summer, he would come up for weekends and for his two-week vacation. His visits were eagerly anticipated. He would show up with toys and comic books, drive us to the nearest town for grocery shopping and ice cream, and hold us up on the surface of the water while we learned to swim.

Mom's jobs didn't vary much from what they were back in the city: fix meals, wash clothes, clean up, and try to enforce some minimal rules of behavior. She never got as much appreciation as Dad.

Jeannette and me being bratty in the Catskills with Ira and Mom.

Why the Catskills?

Toward the end of the nineteenth century, Jewish farmers purchased land in the Catskills and built summer resorts. By the 1950s around half a million New Yorkers, mostly Jews, had taken to spending the sweltering months in what came to be known as the "Borscht Belt." Jews were welcome there, unlike most places in the Unites States, where anti-Semitism prevailed.

Although air-conditioning was widely available, it was still beyond the means of the average worker. In 1952 a 5,500 BTU unit (one that could cool a 10x10 bedroom) cost $350. We would have needed three of them to ameliorate summers in our tiny ground-floor apartment, and they would be useless the rest of the year. Just one would likely have blown the 15-amp fuses in our apartment (15 amps were standard at the time). But even if the fuse held, our electricity bill would blast through the ceiling and the roof as well. Air-conditioning wasn't an option, given my father's take-home pay of seventy dollars per week. These summers in the Catskills were more affordable.

There were roughly three levels of accommodation in the Borscht Belt. The most expensive was one of the fancy hotels, like the Concord or Grossinger's. For that you got three kosher meals per day, maid service, entertainment at the nightclub, and a huge indoor swimming pool.

The least expensive was the *kuchalein* (cook alone), a boardinghouse where you could rent one or two bedrooms upstairs and had to share a bath with the other boarders. Downstairs was a large shared kitchen. Every mother cooked alone for her children, but then they ate with everyone else at the same time in a central dining room. Allan Warshawsky, a longtime friend and Gay Liberation Front member, says his family sometimes stayed in these. They got two burners on one of the ranges and half a refrigerator: "You can imagine the fights: that was my milk, the range is so dirty, everything you put in the fridge goes bad and stinks, etc."

The middle level of accommodation in the Borscht Belt was a bungalow. Since my father was a civil servant, we were able to stay in these. They cost around $200 for the entire summer. Dad's steady job allowed him to take out a loan at 3 percent in May and pay it off over the cooler months, just in time to reapply the following May. For that $200 we had access to farm-fresh food, a swimming hole, and meadows to play on instead of concrete and asphalt. And clean air! In the evenings we sat out on the lawn and watched glorious sunsets. At night we gazed at the uncountable stars and the band of the Milky Way stretching across the sky. In those days, back in New York, coal furnaces heated the city, and its sky always had a gray tinge. I never saw stars there outside the Hayden Planetarium, or a colorful sunset except in paintings at the museum, or even a rainbow.

Cows, Snakes, and Voodoo Dolls

I don't remember all the dinky hamlets where we stayed, but Ellenville was one—called "Socconessing" by its original inhabitants. The word means "a muddy place where the water comes out," and its residents included thick swarms of mosquitoes. In my mind's eye I can still see our neighbors in the next bungalow, their legs decorated with sores where they'd scratched themselves bloody. Fireflies also loved the place. Ignorant of their needs, I put some in a jar without holes in the lid for oxygen. They were dead by morning.

Another of the colonies was down the road from a berry farm. When the blueberries ripened, Mom grabbed some pots and a couple of jugs of water, and we went picking. We also collected apples. Mom canned the fruits and used them for pies back in the city.

The summers when I was ten and eleven, we rented one of the bungalows at Mayberg's Colony in Harris, New York. I haven't found midcentury census data for Harris, but most recently it had a resident population of sixty-nine. The only amenities were a post office and a convenience store.

Mayberg's was next door to a kuchalein, and Jeannette made friends with two girls who stayed there. It was also adjacent to a small dairy farm. The barn was down the road, maybe a couple city blocks away, while the pasture ran over the hills and above the bungalows. Mom used to carry a couple of bottles to the barn every morning at milking time, and the owner would fill them directly from a cow's teat. The milk wasn't pasteurized, but the cows were tuberculin tested. It wasn't homogenized either, so Mom would pour off half the cream, saving it for coffee, and then shake up the bottle whenever a child wanted a drink.

Most days the kids in the colony played outside, lightly super-vised if at all—unless we were going swimming. Favorite games were ringolevio—a form of tag—and a vicious card game called knucks. The winners got to whack the loser on the knuckles with the deck of cards.

I often wandered off by myself. Fascinated by the cows, I'd duck through the barbed wire fence and enter their pasture to observe them, from a safe distance. Sometimes I drew them. The younger kids found cow patties more intriguing than bovine anatomy and used sticks to fling bits of dung at each other.

I'd always been interested in science, even as a small child. I'd read somewhere that part of scientific training involved dissecting a frog, so I caught a hapless amphibian and cut it open. Needless to say, I didn't learn anything—except to regret it, along with the dead fireflies, to this day.

Perhaps because the environment was safer for their children, our mothers seemed more relaxed in the country. Occasionally they sat together and knitted garments for winter. Mom made a couple of beautiful sweaters for me, one the color of milk chocolate and the other Persian blue with two rows of red stars across the chest. She tried teach-ing me to knit, but I was recalcitrant. I was bored by the work, and by sitting around with adult women when I wanted to run and play.

Sometimes a foursome got together for mah-jongg. One of those afternoons, I was aimlessly wandering in the thick grass at the edge of the lawn when I spotted a couple of black snakes. I knew that these weren't poisonous, so I grabbed them by their necks and headed toward the women. "Ma! Look what I got!"

The three women ran off as fast as they could, leaving my mother to deal with me. "Throw those things away!" she shouted, her face red with what must have been a mixture of anger and fear.

I complied, though just a little regretful at not being able keep these new pets. Mostly, however, I felt tremendously proud. I'd scared away grownups who didn't know the difference between the nonvenomous black snakes and rattlers or copperheads.

Another episode of childhood arrogance: Anita, the fourteen-year-old granddaughter of the Maybergs, was nasty to us younger kids. I made a plasticine voodoo doll to represent her and stuck a pin in it. When she found out, she grew very distressed and developed a headache. One of the other adults, probably Anita's mother, told my mother, who ordered me to squish the doll. When I complied, the headache went away. Again I was filled with pride. I didn't believe in voodoo or any kind of magic, but this stupid girl—three years older than I was—did!

That same year I became friends with nine-year-old Roberta. I'd heard there was a waterfall at the end of a nearby dirt road and decided that we should go see it. This may have been the first time that I demonstrated any leadership skills, and Roberta was quite willing to follow. The road, which hadn't been used in many seasons, had potholes the size of basketballs. We passed a decaying farmhouse, which we'd been told was haunted. We peeked into the cracked windows but didn't try to go in. Four miles later we came to a small waterfall. At the end of a fairly dry summer the flow was so diminished that we could hear a car approaching behind us.

"You two get in!" Dad yelled. He was pretty upset. "I almost busted an axle going down this road." He never told me how he knew where we were going, or how frightened he must have been for our safety.

The next expedition I instigated was to Monticello, the big town in the area. In 1955 it had around forty-seven hundred residents. Monticello boasted a supermarket and stores that sold various necessities to summer people, such as bathing suits and the colorful swim tubes that fit around a child's waist. Of most interest to us, it had ice cream.

Roberta and I hiked the 6.5 miles to Monticello and went directly to the ice cream parlor. Afterward, too tired to walk home, we stood by the side of the road and stuck our thumbs out. A nice guy drove us all the way back to the bungalows. Two little girls, an eleven-year-old and a nine-year-old, hitchhiking . . . our parents were not pleased. I suppose they clamped down, as I don't remember any further such adventures.

That was our last summer in the bungalow colonies. The next year they sent us to sleepaway camp.

4

RACE, AND THE
RACE TO SPACE

I HAD ALMOST EVERYTHING I wanted as a child—except for a dog and a telescope. It was impossible to keep four people and a dog in a one-bedroom apartment. I got a hamster. Jeannette got a parakeet, and we had goldfish. My parents said a telescope was too expensive, but they did buy me a child's chemistry set. The instruction booklet told you how to do "experiments" with household items, like mixing baking soda and vinegar. Those didn't seem like experiments to me, just recipes, as the booklet already told you what the outcome would be. One of the recipes involved heating ingredients over a candle flame. I was sitting on the kitchen floor, trying to read the instructions and perform the procedure at the same time, and the booklet caught fire. Mom shouted, "You're going to burn the house down," and stamped it out. The chemistry set disappeared after that.

Mom wanted to give us all the advantages she didn't have, so she bought a secondhand upright piano. The day it was delivered our neighbors came in and looked it over, just as though it had been a new baby, although they didn't make cooing noises. I don't think anyone else in the building had one. My sister and I had to take lessons. The local teacher charged only two or three dollars and came to our apartment, but Mom saw pretty quickly that she wasn't very good and started taking us to

Mr. Fichandler in Manhattan. His lessons were five dollars. I disliked practicing and never became proficient. Mom also brought me to the Metropolitan Opera House for ballet lessons, but after a few of these I revolted, sitting down on the curb and refusing to go.

We rode the subway for both sets of lessons, with lunch at the Automat as a special treat. I loved putting nickels in the vending machines and always ordered a frankfurter. We had to eat the creamed spinach, which wasn't too bad, and then got cherry pie for dessert.

In 1953, when I was nine, we moved to a larger apartment, three blocks away. While Mom was caring for my sister and me in the Catskills, Dad made the arrangements. He hadn't consulted with her and, according to Jeannette, she was pretty upset. The building was run-down. It wasn't quite a slum—there were no rats or roaches—though Dad used to joke that the landlady would make repairs by picking up a fallen piece of plaster, spitting on it, and slapping it back into the hole in the wall. Our new place had three bedrooms—the large one for Mom and Dad and the two tiny ones for my sister and me.

Acquiring a Brother

Around the same time as we moved to the new apartment, Cousin Ira, who had spent summers with us in the Catskills, came to live with us permanently.

Ira's mother—my mother's sister Rosa—was, according to my mother, "retarded." Mom told my sister that Rosa was "emotionally disturbed." Looking back on it, I doubt if either label was true. None of the Bojankosky kids received more than a few years of elementary education in Havana, yet all of them, as adults, were fluent in Yiddish, Spanish, and English. Lacking formal schooling, Rosa could only find work in factories.

When she came of age she married Miguel Terman, a Peruvian, and gave birth to Ira. Miguel took the family to Lima—thirty-six hundred miles from anyone Rosa knew. Again, according to my mother's account, when Rosa had marital difficulties she complained to Grandma Leah, who told her to come home. She returned to Brooklyn, bringing the baby with her, and put him in her parents' care while she went to work.

As our grandparents' health declined, Ira was spending much of his time in the streets and increasingly had to take care of himself. I remember being astonished at seeing my little cousin light the gas stove and boil an egg. My sister and I weren't allowed to touch the kitchen matches.

Grandma Leah broke her hip and was no longer able to provide Ira with even minimal care. Fortunately, we had space for him in our new, larger apartment—he slept on a cot in the living room. Our grandparents barely spoke English, and the only reading materials in their home were a Hebrew prayer book and Yiddish newspapers, so Ira's language skills were limited. My parents thought that the best he could hope for would be laboring jobs. They were mistaken. He was valedictorian in high school, and became a mathematician.

My grandparents did love Ira, and that love was reciprocated. As an adult he became engaged to a Norwegian girl and married her in 1975 but never told Grandpa. That would have broken the old man's heart.

I don't know why Rosa entered a second marriage, this time with Sam Grosberg, a Holocaust survivor. The wedding took place in our little apartment. I was given a very important role—playing the first lines of the wedding march on the piano. Soon they had two little boys, David and Joseph. Apparently Sam was abusive, and that marriage broke up as well. Rosa had to return to factory work. Sam raised David, who got away from his father by enlisting as soon as he was of age. My mother couldn't take on any more children in addition to the three she now had, and she was also taking care of her disabled parents, so Joseph went to an orphanage.

I did not get to know Rosa well, as I was pretty self-absorbed during my adolescence and left home as soon as I legally could. My sister stayed close to the family and reports that Rosa was a kind, caring person. She and my father looked after each other when my mother died.

The Love That Didn't Know Its Name

I met Lynne Rutledge around that time as well, when I was nine and in fifth grade, and she became my best friend. She was an only child. Her mother was a math teacher at the local junior high school and her father a probation officer, which meant that both were college graduates. They owned a brownstone house a few blocks to the west, in a nicer neighborhood. Lynne's family was higher class than we were—but lower in caste. They were Black.

We sat together in school. Sometimes Lynne would come to our place for dinner, and then the two of us would adjourn to the living room couch and watch TV, holding hands in the darkened room. My body still remembers the sweet scent of her pomade and the warmth of her fingers caressing mine.

In elementary school we were in the same classroom all day. But once we entered junior high, each subject had a different teacher, and when the bell rang we picked up our books and clattered up or down the steel staircase to the next teacher's room. Since Lynne's mother was our group's math teacher, Lynne had to go to another class for that period. One time as we were about to separate, she leaned over and kissed me on the cheek. That kiss stayed with me all day—it still does.

I was eleven then and had no idea what those feelings were about.

The previous year I'd learned about a legal system set up to hurt the friend I loved so much. Of course, I'd absorbed the caste structure of the United States—from WASP men on top down to Black women on the bottom—but I don't remember being aware of conditions in the South until May 17, 1954, when the Supreme Court declared separate schools illegal. The newspaper stories continued, week after week, with readers attacking or defending segregation. The Montgomery bus boycott came in December 1955. The more I read, the more I imagined Lynne in that situation, and I hurt for her.

Both of us were in one of the three "special progress" classes at John Marshall Junior High. (Later the name was changed to Mary McLeod Bethune Middle School, to honor the daughter of slaves rather than a slaveholder.) It meant that we went directly from seventh to ninth grade, finishing the required work in two years instead of three. Lynne was the only Black student in our class. The ethnic composition of the school as a whole during those years was 45 percent White, 45 percent Black, and 10 percent Puerto Rican.

Since I was supposed to have a boyfriend, I hung out with Irwin Rothenberg. What brought us together were interests in science—me in astronomy, him in meteorology—rather than any romantic feelings. I danced with him at the junior high prom.

On a spring day, a few months after I'd turned twelve, I met Lynne at the park. She was there with two other Black girls from the regular classes, playing on the jungle gym. The three of them swung over the pipes and hung head down from their knees. I wouldn't do it. I wasn't much of an athlete. I'd learned to roller-skate and ride a bike but got seasick on a park swing and hated being upside down. The girls derided me for being unable to do it—even Lynne. Feeling betrayed, I blurted, "At least my hair's prettier than yours!"

The minute those words came out of my mouth I knew I'd said something unforgivable. I don't remember what happened the rest of that day, but I guess Lynne did forgive me, because we stayed friends.

The others didn't let it go, though. Not long after that incident in the park, I was hospitalized with acute appendicitis. In those days they didn't discharge patients as quickly as possible, but kept me for a week. For another week or two, while my abdomen was healing, I had to wear a girdle. The first day I returned to school those girls found me and punched me in the belly. It didn't hurt all that much, but I was pretty scared.

I felt too vulnerable to fight back. Instead, I told my homeroom teacher, and she notified the dean of girls, who called us into her office. Miss Schanz was big and tall. We called her a horse behind her back. That day, she chewed my assailants out. Then she said she'd teach them how it felt and punched one of them in the belly. I was horrified. NYC public school teachers weren't allowed to hit kids, and I knew she wouldn't have done it, wouldn't have thought she could get away with it, if the girls were White. From that day on I hated Miss Schanz.

Flunking Housework, and Early Motherhood

One of our fifth-grade homework assignments had been to sew an apron and bring it to class by the end of the term. Only the girls had to do that. I don't know what the boys were expected to do. I happily did my academic work but wouldn't touch needle and thread—sewing was just as boring as the knitting Mom had tried to teach me in the Catskills.

Finally, the day before we were supposed to bring the aprons in, Mom ran the hated garment off on her sewing machine. The teacher accepted my apron without a word. One day she commented disapprovingly, in front of the whole class, that Martha didn't like working with her hands.

That wasn't true. Although Mom could never get me to wash dishes, sweep, mop, cook (except for chocolate pudding), or do most of the other chores considered "women's work," I didn't mind vacuuming, cleaning the Venetian blinds, or washing windows. Perhaps they seemed like boy chores, or at least neutral.

Motherhood wasn't on my agenda, either. That same year, when I was twelve and Mom was forty-two, we had a mysterious conversation. She asked me if I'd be willing to take care of a baby brother or sister. My obvious disinterest confirmed what she already knew, and she didn't bring the subject up again. Shortly thereafter she spent a couple of days in the hospital, but never told us kids why.

It took me decades to figure out what had happened. Either she thought she was past menopause, or the contraception failed. She had three children and two increasingly disabled parents to care for and, due to the poor nutrition of her childhood, wasn't in the best of health herself. She'd had two miscarriages before I showed up and she loved children, which was why she hoped against hope that I would suddenly develop a maternal instinct. But after that conversation, she called Dr. Warwick. He had delivered me and my sister and had cared for Mom throughout the years.

The D&C he performed was, of course, illegal at the time.

A Rocket That Fizzled

During the 1950s, even before Sputnik, the United States was sending rockets into space, sometimes with a couple of unlucky mice or hamsters as passengers. This inspired high school students around the country to launch homemade rockets. It inspired a few younger kids as well.

Four of us from the gifted class—Alan Silberman, Allan Warshawsky, Lynne, and I—met at the Silberman house. Alan's older brother was studying chemistry in college and kept some equipment in the basement, including a rabbit in a cage and some pet mice. Our plan was to build a rocket and send one of the mice up into the stratosphere. My father had a chemical dictionary, sitting next to the encyclopedia volumes he'd purchased on the installment plan. I copied the recipe for gunpowder and brought it to Alan's basement. We made some from Alan's brother's supplies, rolled it up in a paper napkin, put it under a cone made of aluminum foil, and lit one end of the paper with a match. The results were disappointing. The gunpowder roll burned but the cone stayed on the ground. Our little bit of learning hadn't included the fact that gunpowder requires pressure to explode, and we thought we'd gotten the formula wrong. We were too ignorant to know that we had dodged a very real bullet, sparing our fingers, our eyes, and a mouse's life.

That same year I took a test for admission to a specialized school, the Bronx High School of Science. It was the only science-related school in New York that accepted girls. When the letter saying I'd passed arrived in the mail, my mother was beside herself with joy— she practically danced in the kitchen. I was the only kid from Brooklyn admitted that year, most likely because hardly any applied. The commute was too long. Lynne went on to Erasmus Hall in Brooklyn. Irwin got into Stuyvesant, an all-boys science and math school in lower Manhattan.

During my first year at Science High, I walked ten blocks to the subway station, took the train to the Bronx, and then walked a little farther to the school door, an hour and a half each way. I could do some homework on the train, but I always had more to do at night. I had no time for old friends and eventually lost touch with most of them. I always wondered what happened to Lynne.

———————

Both my parents were passionate about education. My father hadn't been able to go to high school during the Depression, but after World War II he took night school classes and passed the GED, which allowed him to leave the ammunition factory and get a clerical job. When I was a child, he frequented garage sales and brought home boxes of used books. One year an encyclopedia salesman talked him into purchasing the *Encyclopedia*

Britannica. He took a part-time job, working Friday evenings and part of the weekend, to make the monthly payments.

I'm not sure how much schooling Mom had in Havana before she too was sent to work—my sister thinks she had a year or two of high school. But she was always reading, from the Tolstoy novels I saw on her night table when I was a kid to Jeannette's college textbooks. She'd forgotten what little Polish she knew as a child but was fluent in Yiddish, Spanish, and English. When I entered first grade, I asked her what came next. "After elementary school you go to high school and then college. And then," she added firmly, "you get your PhD."

At other times the plan was for me to get an MD. In any case, her kids were going to college. We couldn't even imagine an alternative.

5

THE BODY ADOLESCENT

MY PARENTS PROVIDED NOTHING in the way of sex education. My earliest memory, in fact, was of being beaten for masturbating. The public schools offered a class called Hygiene, which was supposed to encourage "family life." No information there either.

What I did learn began in second grade: one day when a group of us were in the playground, little Melvin asked if we knew where babies came from. No one answered. Melvin—the shortest kid in class, best hitter in softball practice, foulest mouth—went on to enlighten us. "A man puts his thing in a woman's . . ."

"My parents would never do anything like that," I insisted. But the other kids seemed to believe him. After school I went to my mother for assurance. She didn't utter a word. Her crimson blush said it all—Melvin was right.

Tucked in the bookshelves with the encyclopedia and chemical dictionary was a volume about medicine. It had articles about reproduction and drawings of the pertinent organs. All the other information I got came from my peers, in the form of crude jokes.

As a December baby, I had started kindergarten at age four and a half. Skipping eighth grade meant that I started high school at thirteen. So at the same time as I was losing contact with my friends, I was also suffering the miseries of puberty.

The physical changes of adolescence are hard enough, but in the 1950s were perhaps much harder for a budding lesbian than for my heterosexual contemporaries. I was not at home in my body. Among the pictures I drew and taped to the door of my bedroom was one of a shapeless creature wearing glasses. Below it I wrote, "I am an annoying blob."

The first pubic hair was a tragedy. I was becoming a woman, like it or not, and that meant being consigned to women's roles: cleaning house, waiting on men. Being a woman meant that if you were going out, you had to squash your flesh into bras, girdles, and nylon stockings. You had to hobble around in high heels. You had to pin your hair into hard plastic rollers at night and sleep on them—a form of torture I tried only once or twice, when my kid sister took up the practice.

At either twelve or thirteen I did what many girls that age did: cut myself with a razor. Not very much, maybe three or four times altogether, just enough to feel some pain.

Moving to the Projects

Mom and Dad understood at least part of the problem. Without my knowing it, they had applied for public housing, and at the beginning of my second year at Science High, we moved to the Marble Hill public housing project in the Bronx. Now the bus to school took only half an hour. My parents made the sacrifice: Dad had the long commute, the ninety-minute train ride to his job at the far end of Brooklyn. When Mom needed to look after her disabled parents, she traveled the same distance, back to our old neighborhood.

The Marble Hill housing project was for "middle income" families, meaning those not on welfare. It consisted of eleven buildings, each fourteen or fifteen stories tall, with a total of 1,682 apartments. I thought they looked hideous, like enormous hives for worker bees. The residents were a mix of Jewish, Italian, Irish, Latino, and Black families, and the fathers tended to be employed as lower-grade civil servants, sales clerks, bus or taxi drivers, and such—the kind of jobs you could get without a college degree. Most of the mothers weren't in the paid labor force.

The apartment had only two bedrooms, so I lost what little privacy I'd enjoyed the last couple of years and had to share with Jeannette again. Ira slept in the living room. Mom couldn't get me to do dishes, but I didn't mind cleaning the blinds and washing the windows. We were on the eighth floor. Sometimes I thought about throwing myself out.

The city had planted some patches of lawn around each building, but kids weren't allowed to walk or play on the grass. If we did, our family got a citation—and we could be evicted. What served as a playground was a square of asphalt and concrete, with benches around the perimeter and a kind of concrete step pyramid in the center. I don't know why they put the pyramid there instead of swings or a jungle gym. Sometimes I hung out in the square with the other teens. One evening devil-may-care Joey Gonzalez raced his bicycle around the playground, dashing up to one girl after another and slapping her on the behind. Each girl shrieked and giggled and jumped up on the step pyramid to avoid him, but descended in time for his next charge. I was disgusted. Why were the girls acting like a bunch of ninnies? Why didn't they defend themselves?

When he came at me, I took a wide stance, grabbed the handlebars of the bike, and tossed him to the ground. The other teens gasped and then were silent. I walked off and went home. Throwing Joey off the bike didn't endear me to that crowd—except for Lenny, who stuttered and in retrospect was probably gay. He took me aside and told me that he admired me.

Many years later, when I talked to Jeannette about the incident, she said, "You don't get it. They were flirting." She also commented that Joey Gonzalez was gorgeous and that she and her friends all had crushes on him.

I still don't get it. Why should flirting consist of a boy smacking a girl's ass, and her pretending both pleasure and helplessness?

I don't remember who told me, but there had been quite a number of suicide attempts, and possibly even some successful suicides, at Science High. Most of the kids, like me, had gotten top grades in their junior high school classes. Here we had been thrown in with our intellectual peers, while under intense pressure from ambitious parents to be the best, to get into the best colleges. The teachers had been alerted to keep an eye out for warning signs—and my trigonometry instructor spotted me. I was referred for therapy.

I'm not sure how much good the therapist did, as I was in such psychological pain that I barely said a word during our sessions. But I did start to make friends again, and my life began to improve.

6

OH BABY!

IT WAS A SHORT BUS RIDE to high school once my family moved to the Bronx. By then I was a junior. During the first part of that year, I found myself sitting next to another Science High student, Kazuyo Shiraishi. We didn't talk very much, possibly because she was as shy as I was back then, possibly because her spoken English was limited. But she was obviously bright enough to be accepted to the school. Her father was in some kind of import business, cultured pearls, I think, which was why they lived in New York.

We were in Mrs. Gordon's social studies class. That subject was where you learned the official history of the United States and were fed propaganda about how great our system is. For example, one of the topics in my junior high school social studies class was "Communism vs. Democracy." *Wait a minute*, I thought at the time, *Communism is an economic system. Democracy is a political system. It should be "Communism vs. Capitalism," or "Democracy vs. Dictatorship."* But I didn't challenge the teacher then.

In high school I did: At the end of a lecture about WWII, Mrs. Gordon recounted how our victorious army tried the Japanese generals for war crimes—of course a conviction was foreordained—then hanged them, burned their bodies, and sent the ashes to their families. What got to me was that she seemed to be gloating about it, just as the newspapers had gloated over the execution of the Rosenbergs.

I raised my hand. "I suppose if the Japanese had won, they would have done the same thing to Franklin Roosevelt and our generals."

Mrs. G. turned bright red and shouted, "I never want to hear anyone talk like that again!"

I guess most of the other students had been dozing off and missed my remark. "What did she say?" they asked each other.

At that moment the bell rang, and it was time to go to the next class. I'm sure Mrs. G. had intended to chastise me, but I walked out holding my head up proudly. Thinking back on it, I wonder if she had lost people during that war, maybe a brother or cousin. Perhaps I should have felt compassion for her instead of adolescent self-righteousness.

Not too long after that incident, performers from the Kabuki Theater came to NYC, and Kazuyo's parents invited me to a show. I knew nothing of Japanese culture and had never seen anything like Kabuki—so gorgeous, a wonderful gift. But at the end of the semester, the Shiraishi family returned to Japan, and Kazuyo and I lost touch.

Changing Directions

I loved physics and did well in it. Chemistry lecture came right after lunch, after I'd eaten a full meal and a piece of cafeteria cherry pie, so I tended to doze off. Lab was problematic, since our measuring equipment was shoddy and the experiments never came out right.

Two incidents from biology—where I also did well—stick in my mind. One day we were studying digestion and the teacher had us chant the names of enzymes. I can still hear our ragged little chorus: "pepsin, trypsin, amylopsin!" On another day the same teacher was reprimanding us for something and started to say, "When I was your age . . ."

A young man sitting in the back sang out, "Pass the bread—here comes the baloney!" The teacher threw him out of the room. That young man was Stokely Carmichael. I hadn't particularly noticed him before as I sat up front. But I guess he was allowed to return because he did graduate and went on to Howard University. Next time I heard his name he'd become a leader in the Student Nonviolent Coordinating Committee.

I didn't know how to design experiments on my own and didn't have a mentor who might have guided me into a career in science. What changed my life was Jack Luria's creative writing class. We were allowed to write what came to mind, without much in the way of criticism. Fortunately, none of what I pumped out then has survived. The fragments I do remember were cringeworthy, to say the least.

Five members of that class used to meet in the local pizzeria at the end of the school day. These were Judy Lieberman, Samuel "Chip" Delany, Pat Buchanan, Jeff Borak, and me. We shook oregano and red pepper flakes on our slices and held forth in the way a group of over-intellectualized adolescents do. Well, *I* added red pepper flakes—Judy tried them once and drank lots of water to, as she put it, "get over the shock." She never tried them again. At last I had a gang, a new group of friends to replace those I'd lost in junior high school. Jeff later ran the school's literary magazine, *Dynamo*. Judy was on the staff as well. I don't remember much about Pat, who was very quiet, and don't know what happened to her or to Jeff after graduation.

Judy and I both lusted after Chip. A light-skinned Black boy, he was almost two years older than we were. And handsome, with a dancer's spring in his walk. The only boy I ever had a crush on of course turned out to be gay. He went on to become an award-winning science fiction writer.

Judy (who later changed her name to its Hebrew equivalent, Yehudit) became my best friend. The Liebermans lived in a co-op building in the Morningside Heights neighborhood of upper Manhattan. Like my junior high school friend Lynne, she was an only child, her family middle class. Both her parents were kind and welcoming. Ben Lieberman, tall, lank, and starting to go bald, ran a mail-order book business. I remember him warning us that men were sexual predators and me thinking he was just old and cynical. Esther Lieberman was short, with dark hair, and worked as a math teacher. Her cooking was more Americanized than my immigrant mother's—she introduced me to English muffins.

The Liebermans had joined a socialist group during the Depression, and witnessed the squabbles between Stalinists, Trotskyites, and other factions contending for leadership of a future workers' revolution in the

United States. Judy grew up hearing, and being appalled by, stories of onetime comrades who never spoke to each other again. A girl with a gentle nature, she chose the path of kindness rather than contentiousness.

How wonderful it was to be fifteen, exploring the city—and its windows to a wider world! One day Judy and I took the ferry to Staten Island, which was more rural in those days, and then an hour-long bus ride to Lighthouse Avenue. The driver let us off on a tree-lined dirt road (it's paved now). It had been raining, and we had to step over puddles to reach the Tibetan Museum. Built on a hillside, it was designed to resemble a Tibetan monastery, with priceless art inside and terraced gardens and lotus ponds out back. On another day we saw Ingmar Bergman's most recent film, *The Seventh Seal*, so unlike the Hollywood movies we'd grown up with. On both occasions we were bowled over.

Judy applied to Radcliffe for early admission and was accepted, leaving Science High at the end of our junior year. We corresponded regularly and saw each other when she came home for holidays until she moved to California. She continued studying science and math and worked in computers while playing her violin in university orchestras and other ensembles. When she got her PhD, she found that the only people who wanted to employ her were the Defense Department and large corporations like Standard Oil—institutions she opposed on principle. Even more, those kinds of jobs would require forty to fifty hours per week, leaving no time for the music she loved. After temporizing for a year, she decided to devote herself to her art. Fortunately her husband supported her in this. She studied and practiced for two years and then started auditioning.

While still unsure as to whether she wanted to make such a huge change, she went to dinner with her husband and his sister. "I've put in all this time preparing myself in math and science," she said. "How can I just throw it all away?"

Her sister-in-law replied, "That's what they're saying about the Vietnam War."

That clinched it. Eventually she was accepted into the newly formed San Francisco Ballet Orchestra. For the next fifty years, she enjoyed a career as a professional musician. We are still the closest of friends.

I never considered applying for early admission anywhere and didn't even know it was possible. During my senior year at Science High, I applied to Cornell University's agronomy program. I can't imagine why I thought they might admit me, since I'd never so much as sprouted a bean in a flowerpot. I flubbed the interview at Barnard but did qualify for City College.

The Big Day

June came around. We seniors assembled a couple of times, rehearsing for graduation. Our school song was no less dreadful than others of its kind, though perhaps not quite as wretched as the poetry I wrote in Mr. Luria's class. I'm not sure how many years that anthem had been in use before we had to learn it.

Between the first stanza and the chorus were three transitional rising notes. You couldn't eliminate them, or the music wouldn't work. We were supposed to be silent for those notes, which would be played on the piano. During one of our rehearsals, a student in the back filled the transition, shouting out "Oh bay-bee!" A male voice—I never found out whose, but wouldn't be surprised if it had been Stokely's.

The music teacher had us try again, whereupon the rest of us chimed in, "Oh baby!" The principal was summoned. He told us that we would not be allowed to leave until we performed the song properly. We obeyed. It was late in the afternoon, and we wanted to go home. Besides, we were good kids. Hard workers. Bright, ambitious, destined to make our marks in the world.

The long-awaited day finally arrived. We filled the front rows of the auditorium, our families the rear. At the end of the ceremony, after we suffered through the guest speaker, a diplomat from India who blathered on interminably while we folded our programs into paper airplanes and launched them, after the diplomas and awards were handed out, the principal addressed our parents. He informed them that we were no longer students but alumnae now, and were no longer his responsibility. "And now, let's sing!"

You know what happened next.

Such was the extent of our rebellion in 1960. The mass movements of the '60s were yet to come: the Freedom Rides began in 1961, the anti–Vietnam War protests in 1963. But I understand that after we mangled the anthem, the music teacher composed a different one for the next graduating class. One without those damned transitional notes.

7

WHEN COLLEGE
WAS FREE

In 1960, at the age of sixteen, I entered the City College of New York. It offered both bachelor's and graduate degrees, providing an education that many considered on a par with the Ivy League. However, it was a big impersonal institution, and I never did make friends there; I was never part of a gang, as I had been in junior high and high school.

I remember my expenses as around $230 per year, which must have covered fees and books. My sister, who entered college three years later, tells me her registration fee was seventeen dollars. Tuition was free. Since I lived at my parents' home during the first couple of years, room and board were free as well.

With no idea of a long-term goal, I tried various subjects.

First, the sciences. I have delightful memories of field trips to watch the emergence of horseshoe crabs at a beach in the Bronx and to observe the geology of cliffs in New Jersey. We were lectured on DNA, the new hot topic in biology. But just as in high school, I didn't have a mentor or get to do any real experiments. My childhood dreams of a scientific career—or by then, the remnants of such dreams—evaporated.

Next I tried math. Calculus was intriguing, but in the long run I found statistics most useful. It came in handy a few years later when, as the speaker for Daughters of Bilitis, I had to explain to kids in an abnormal psych class that being *abnormal* means only you're at one of the thin ends of a bell curve, away from the central hump where most people cluster. It's not a synonym for *diseased*. I also learned (as my wife, Sylvia, now puts it) that my chances of winning the lottery are pretty much the same whether I buy a ticket or not. In general, though, math was too abstract for me to consider it as a major.

I liked to draw and was pretty good at it, so I tried taking art classes. Once my kid sister told me that if I became an artist, I would have to live in a garret and cut off my ear. She needn't have worried. One instructor told us to appreciate those great examples of twentieth-century art, the highway clover leaf and the George Washington Bridge. Another invited me to admire his work, which consisted of pipes welded together. They looked as though they had been salvaged from drains in a demolished building. Maybe this was the kind of art our society valued at the time, but it didn't call to me.

About halfway through college, I had my first affair with a woman who encouraged me to get into Sullivanian therapy. While hanging out with other people in that form of therapy, I considered becoming a psychologist. I took classes in the social sciences. In those prefeminist days, the textbooks made dutiful obeisance to Freud and Adler and their ilk. More interesting was a field trip to the state hospital, where I played pool with residents on the schizophrenic ward. One old woman sat in a chair and said nothing, but the others seemed no crazier than the rest of us.

Since I was just coming out, I made a quiet visit to the psych department library and read journal articles about homosexuality. The majority of the authors wrote about gays as if we were insects on a dissecting tray. Some writers were downright prurient. I hated them, yet their contempt seeped in and left me feeling like some kind of unwholesome freak. In the end, though, I accumulated enough credits in sociology, psychology, and anthropology for them to count as part of a social science major.

I eventually graduated with a double major, the other in literature. Some faculty members in that field were enthusiastic about their subjects, and I responded in kind. I enjoyed learning a bit of Old English but found Beowulf tedious. Another hero slays another dragon—yawn.

I loved Chaucer and really took a shine to the Wyfe of Bath, feeling that I had a lot in common with this character, including a gap between our front teeth. The poets Whitman and Dickinson were also favorites. I knew they both were gay, though the teacher insisted there was no evidence of it.

A few instructors were dreadful. If you want to kill any interest in Shakespeare, teach him the way our instructor did: for practically every class, make us read a play at home and take a test on various details the following day. No dramatic readings, nothing but tests. Another teacher—I'll call him Mr. Farley—asked us who we thought was the greatest American writer. "Mark Twain?" a student suggested.

"No, it was Henry James," Mr. Farley replied, serenely. (*Well, la-di-da!* I thought. James wrote about the upper classes and eventually became a British citizen.) Farley went on to brag about having been to tea with the British ambassador.

One teacher in the English department—I'll call him Mr. Warner—used crutches as a result of contracting polio as a child. The day after the 1964 Republican convention, he hauled himself in and sat down. Instead of going over whatever the original assignment had been, he began to rant. Even if I had owned a TV at the time, I wouldn't have watched it, but I knew that they had nominated Goldwater. I later learned that the KKK had demonstrated on Goldwater's behalf. Journalist Belva Davis recounted that attendees had chased her and another Black reporter out of the convention hall, shouting racial slurs. Mr. Warner was furious. He described the scene, down to the shower of gold-coin confetti that descended on the frenzied crowd. When he was done, he slammed his fist on the desk and yelled, "Class dismissed!"

I was astounded. Our other instructors hadn't thought, or lacked the courage, to deviate from their usual lesson plans. Mr. Warner, with his atrophied legs, had taken a stand.

My one triumph came in a short-story writing class. Each student had to read his or her work before the rest, who would then critique it. That year I was also studying judo and wrote a tale about a young judoka and his Japanese sensei. The teacher called me in to his office. He insisted that a woman couldn't write from a male point of view—never mind that men have written women's lives for millennia. Instead of letting me present my piece, he read it to the class himself. My classmates liked it—no negative comments. He then asked if any had detected an "off" note. No one had. He tried again, dropping the pronoun *she* with reference to the author. No one had suspected.

He gave me an A for the story, and for my final grade.

8

ARE YOU NOW OR
WERE YOU EVER?

Are you now or were you ever a member of the Communist Party? The Ku Klux Klan? The Nazi Party? The National Negro Labor Council or the Ukrainian-American Fraternal Union? The application for federal employment listed three hundred subversive organizations. I'd heard of the first three but none of the others and, as far as I knew, had never met any of their members.

It was the summer of 1961, and I had just finished my first year at City College. I was seventeen and a loner. I hadn't even belonged to any student clubs. I checked the *No* box. Same with the question about whether I was a homosexual. I'd never met one of those either. Again I checked *No*. I had raging hormones and confused fantasies but was clueless about sexuality in general. Kissing a boy in a movie theater was just a matter of hot saliva, slithery tongues, and his wire braces. What was it supposed to feel like?

Finally, I was advised that the FBI would conduct a background check and might interrogate anyone who knew me. I signed and handed the papers back to Mr. Onorato, the head of the personnel department.

As soon as the spring semester ended, my father had announced that it was time I earned my keep. No more idle, delectable summers on the beach.

Dad took me in to apply. That morning I stuffed my hips into a girdle (skinny girls could make do with a garter belt), legs into nylons, feet into three-inch heels. Smeared deodorant in armpits. Shrugged into a dress. Once I was presentable, Dad escorted my reluctant adolescent self to the Navy Regional Accounts Office—the NRAO—in Brooklyn, where he'd been clerking since the end of World War II.

Now I had that long commute again, an hour and a half from the Bronx to Brooklyn. The subway car was packed, a steam sauna redolent of perfume, sweat, and metabolized alcohol oozing from the drunk hovering over me. The trains weren't air-conditioned in those years.

From the exit it was a two-block trot to the six-story edifice that housed the US Navy's business operations. There was no air-conditioning here either. Fans and fluorescent lights hummed overhead. It smelled of metal desks and stale cigarette smoke.

Victor Onorato was a dapper man with an olive complexion and a serious face. After a brief glance at my completed application, he gave me a typing test. I was sure I'd failed to make thirty-five words per minute, but he passed me. I think he must have owed my father a favor. Then I was sent to the nurse's station, where a med tech tried to test for syphilis. I had small veins. He poked three times without success. "Oh, forget it. You're Jack's kid. You're OK."

On Monday I reported as assigned. My job was to type invoices for all the navy's purchases, covering everything from a $3 million airplane to 144 gross boxes of yo-yos. Did bored sailors have yo-yo contests at sea? I never found out. Another mysterious item was meprobamate— invoices for thousands of tablets every day. Much later, I learned that it was generic for Milltown, the first tranquilizer. I wondered if the entire navy was being treated for psychological disorders.

My hips were trapped under the desk for the eight-hour shift, except for two fifteen-minute breaks and a half-hour lunch in the cafeteria. The girdle and the desk seemed to have been designed as a chastity belt, to anesthetize—if not totally destroy—the life force in my loins.

I was the youngest in the typing pool, surrounded by middle-aged women who chain-smoked constantly. Within a few hours the fumes had made me sick. The supervisor moved me to the back of the room; the draft from the fans carried the smoke toward the front windows. My coworkers never looked up, never said a word to me all summer. I didn't approach them either.

By 5:00 PM on a sweltering summer's day, moisture-laden clouds had eclipsed the sun. We all punched out just as the thunderstorm began and raced to the subway, holding newspapers above our heads to keep from getting drenched, trying desperately to avoid stepping in a grate and breaking a heel. By the time I got home my inner thighs were raw from the girdle.

Although many offices used electric typewriters, the government hadn't upgraded, and we still worked on manual ones. Every night that first week, I kept hearing the *click-click-click* and the *bing!* of the carriage return in my dreams. If I hadn't really been able to type thirty-five words per minute at the beginning of summer, I certainly could at the end. And then it was September and the fall semester had started. I left the NRAO, agreeing to return the following June.

9

WRESTLING WITH WOMEN

I BEGAN MY SOPHOMORE YEAR at City College of New York, having learned two things: I could earn enough to support myself, and I wanted to leave home.

In 1961 my net pay was seventy-six dollars per week. The rule back then was that housing should take no more than 25 percent of your gross income. (At the time of this writing it's gone up to 40 percent, and about one fourth of tenants nationwide are paying over 50 percent.) My week's pay of seventy-six dollars would cover a month's rent on a small apartment in one of the city's shabbier neighborhoods. Nothing fancy, but not a rat-infested slum either. But when I brought up the idea of getting my own apartment, my parents nixed it. It was too dangerous, they said, for a girl to live alone.

My dream of independence went dormant until a month later, when I saw a two-line notice in the *New York Post*. The first all-women's judo class in the city would be held at the YWCA on Fifty-Third and Lexington. The initial series of ten self-defense classes was twenty-seven dollars.

The thought of learning self-defense wasn't completely new to me. Among the books my father had stashed in the basement was a military text with a chapter on hand-to-hand combat. I was fascinated by the drawings and descriptions, but couldn't imagine when I'd find it necessary to sneak up on an enemy sentry and garrote him. Now the training that would enable me to survive on my own was practically at my doorstep—and I wouldn't have to enlist in the military!

I was somewhat apprehensive though. I'd never been inside a YWCA. My parents had raised me in a cultural ghetto—as much as that was possible in NYC. They'd sent me to Jewish summer camps. Would I have to be Christian to join the Y? Would the staff try to convert me? And eighteen was the minimum age to register for judo. I wouldn't hit that mark until winter break. I decided to take the chance. The lady who registered me didn't ask to see ID when I filled out the form, setting my birth date a year earlier. I was in.

Those ten classes were a revelation: our sensei, Ruth Horan, started us easy, teaching us how to escape when someone grabs your wrist, then both wrists, then how to escape from a choke or an attempted rape, and eventually progressing to defenses against knife attacks. No matter how large your opponent, you could still defeat him using leverage and the body's weak points. At the end of the series, we had a test—Horan would launch a surprise attack, and the student had to counter. After passing the introductory course, we could sign up for regular judo classes. I was completely hooked. The rest of my life seemed dull by comparison. During judo my body came alive.

I loved the judo uniform, especially the loose trousers and the low gusset in the crotch that permitted such freedom of movement. I thought it insane that people didn't dress for comfort all the time—that women had to wear girdles, nylons, and high heels. (Nowadays, except for special occasions, I spend most of my waking hours in martial arts trousers.)

During the next few weeks, we learned to fall correctly so that we could practice throwing each other. It was another revelation: I could hurl myself into the air, or be hurled by someone else, and come down unhurt. It was like flying—at least for a second. We paired off by size and wrestled each other on the mat, learning pins and escapes from pins.

By then something dormant in my soul had also come alive. I began to fantasize about the instructor—despite the fact that Ruth was married and her husband, Nick, was the "fall guy," a large man who was kind

Judo demonstration, 1962. I'm sitting on the left. In those days we had to get dolled up and look feminine so as not to scare off the public.

enough to let us practice techniques on him. My infatuation must have been pretty obvious because Louva Irvine, the student I paired up with most often, commented disparagingly about it when we rode the subway home after class. Our teacher didn't deserve that much admiration, she said. She was no genius. Her clothing was way out of date—she still wore seamed nylon stockings. And so on.

In fact, Ruth was a powerhouse, though I didn't know it at the time. She'd worked as an engineer before committing herself full time to teaching self-defense and judo at various locations, including to the New York City meter maids. She also had been a singer, probably with Nick's jazz band during the war years.

Louva's apartment was on the Upper West Side. She exited the train at 110th Street and I continued to the Bronx. During our conversations she told me that she had married right after high school to escape an abusive family. At age twenty-three, after her husband did his military service and they returned to New York, she enrolled at City College.

I was delighted to find another judo student who shared my intellectual interests. We began to meet in the campus cafeteria and then, as the days grew longer, on the lawn. We compared notes on our classes, rated our professors, and shared our ambitions—mine to write books, hers to paint or make films. Louva confessed that she'd never been in love with her husband and was now having an extramarital affair with another CCNY student.

I too had started an affair. My boyfriend of the moment was Patrick Fitzgerald, a young man I'd met a party. Green eyes, very handsome, and very Irish. My mother was appalled when she heard about him. She took to listening in on the extension phone and searching my dresser drawers. I insisted that I was still a virgin, but life at home was becoming increasingly uncomfortable.

In fact, I'd lost my virginity two years earlier. Like most young women of my generation, I knew the mechanics of reproduction but very little else. Both the marriage manuals and the novels I'd read made a big deal about sex but were confusing, so I decided on an experiment—a rather cold-blooded one at that. I picked a guy and lost my virginity in a drive-in movie. Except for a sharp but transient pain, it felt like nothing. At home I looked in the mirror and saw no difference. By the time I met Patrick I'd learned a bit more. Sex with him was pleasant, though not passionate.

I did know enough to protect myself by buying a five-and-dime "wedding" ring and going to the Margaret Sanger Institute for birth control. They fitted me with a diaphragm.

One April evening Louva invited me to her place for dinner. The appetizer was Camembert cheese on crackers. Cheese at home was always the processed kind, American or Swiss, bland and rubbery. I hadn't known that other varieties existed, certainly none so fragrant, sensual to the point of decadence. I don't remember what else we had for dinner, but shortly after the table was cleared Louva's husband came home. A civil engineer, he'd been on the job since 5:00 AM. He went to bed immediately, exhausted. Louva and I continued our conversation in the living room. She suggested practicing the hypnotic techniques her extramarital boyfriend had taught her.

We stretched out on the carpet. She tried to put me in a trance, and then I did the same to her. I had no idea whether we were successful, but when she was "coming out of it" I asked what was on her mind.

"I'm in love with you, you nut!" she exclaimed.

Lips met and opened to hot, wet tongues embracing, exploring the caves of our mouths. Kissing boys had never been anything like this. We fumbled under each other's blouses, down each other's trousers, not daring to strip, whispering so as not to wake her husband.

It was still only an appetizer, not a meal, but I went home on fire, unable to sleep, rolling the word *lesbian* over and over in my mind, telling myself in that overdramatic adolescent way that I'd go through the fires of hell for such kisses. I was in love.

The morning after my first awkward lovemaking with Louva, I called her and told her about my revelation that I was a lesbian. She pooh-poohed me. She didn't want to label herself or our relationship. I was hurt, like a rebuffed puppy. I could hardly take my eyes off her in our next judo class. She was my height, her figure halfway between trim and curvaceous, with dark brown, nearly black hair and a fair Scottish complexion. Her eyes were dark as well, while the whites had an almost bluish cast. What I found most attractive were her crisp walk and gestures, which gave the impression that she might have been a dancer.

About a week later I received a letter from my boyfriend, Patrick—a brief note, actually, written in a crude hand. He had been arrested for shoplifting and would be serving thirty days on Rikers Island. Since I had a spare key, he asked me to look after his apartment.

The truth was, I really didn't know much about him. When I'd asked what he did for work, he said he was a troubleshooter. I assumed that meant some kind of engineer, hired to solve problems in construction or manufacturing. Such was my ignorance and naïveté. It hadn't occurred to me that a guy my own age—eighteen—would hardly qualify for such a position, or that an engineer would probably be occupying something nicer than a basement studio in a run-down building just south of the

Garment District. After reading his note, though, I suspected that he might not even have completed high school.

I told Louva about the apartment right away. She had wanted to leave her husband for some time and seized the opportunity. She packed and moved in, intending to use Patrick's place as a quick transition to a place of her own.

The studio was most likely illegal. It was a few flimsy walls carving out what basement space remained between the furnace and the laundry room. Dark even in the daytime, it had a double bed, clothes closet, and kitchenette. Louva decided to compensate Patrick for use of the space by scrubbing the dirty skillet he'd left in the sink. She washed and dried her linens in the laundry room, put them on the mattress, and invited to me "come wrinkle a sheet." The sheets were cornflower blue, which seemed exotic compared to the plain white linens at home, and were infused with the scent of Tide detergent—a fragrance that became a turn-on during the months of my infatuation. I made love to her. She didn't reciprocate.

Louva found her own apartment quickly enough and was out of Patrick's before he was released. When he came home, he told me that he'd met a couple of guys at Rikers who were going to "teach him the ropes." At this point I broke up with him. I told him, rather priggishly, that I didn't want to be his gun moll.

About a year later, I ran into him on the subway. We didn't say much, but I could tell he was still angry with me. I don't know what direction his life took.

———————

Louva and I continued seeing each other. Since my mother got upset when I didn't come home, I'd put Louva on the phone to prove that I was just spending the night at a girlfriend's house and not with a man. Meanwhile, my world was expanding. Louva introduced me to Scottish folk songs, and we'd dance around her living room. We went to cultural events within our budget, the most memorable being a Miriam Makeba show at the Village Gate.

After she left her husband, Louva stopped going to martial arts. I missed wrestling with her. One evening after class I went to dinner with another judo student. A couple of drinks in, perhaps because Charlene was amiable and I needed a friend, or perhaps because she was Black and knew what it was like to be scorned, I confessed to her that I was having an affair with a woman.

"Welcome to the club!" Charlene's smile was warm and hearty, though with a sad edge. "There's me, and Betty, and Judy, and . . ." She named about half the class. I was completely astonished. Like so many other young gays, I'd been thinking I was the only one. Then Charlene extracted a photo from her wallet, of herself and the famous pop singer Johnny Mathis. "We go out together whenever he needs a pretend girl-friend." (Mathis didn't come out publicly until 1982. When he did, he received death threats, and fell silent about the matter until 2006.)

That year I met Louva's mother, a beaten-down old woman, shapeless, in a faded print housedress. She barely acknowledged my presence. Her husband had been a drunk and occasionally used her as a punching bag. I later realized that he had probably sexually abused Louva as well. But in 1962 nobody talked about that, and I was young and ignorant enough to believe that my love plus a few sessions of therapy would overcome any damage she might have sustained in childhood. Still, there were signs, if I'd been able to read them, that she was living with trauma.

Louva would sleep through the alarm clock and miss work, so she paid an answering service to keep phoning her until she got up. There were piles of laundry in the living room when I visited her, as well as dirty dishes and half-finished cups of coffee scattered about. Some of the latter had been sitting long enough to grow multicolored circles of mold. At the time I thought this meant that Louva had liberated herself from the shackles of housework, and I even admired her for being willing to thumb a nose at society's expectations.

We were sitting on the campus lawn late that spring when I spotted a four-leaf clover, and a moment later saw another. Wanting to share the luck, I offered one to Louva. She refused it. I still don't know why.

As summer approached, she got the idea of applying for a job waiting tables at one of the Catskill Mountain resorts. I applied too, hoping to be with her, but neither of us was hired. I went back to my typing job at the Navy Regional Accounts Office.

———————

In 2005 my wife, Sylvia, and I went to NYC. During that trip we visited the YWCA. The building had been sold to developers, and no one was there except a receptionist and a security guard. We talked our way in, but if we had waited another week, it would have been gone. The gym on the fifth floor still had judo mats hanging on the walls. Above those were HVAC ducts with torn fiberglass insulation hanging down in rags, reminding me of giant versions of the spiderwebs in Miss Havisham's room in *Great Expectations*.

Ruth Horan wrote a book on judo and self-defense for women. I used it after Trump was elected, when a neighbor asked me to teach her little girls how to protect themselves. In later years Ruth retired to Florida, where she taught self-defense to the elderly. She died in 2014 at the age of ninety-one.

10

THERESA SAVES MY ASS

FOR MY SECOND SUMMER at the NRAO I was assigned to a smaller pool, in contracts. Here the girls were my own age and none of them smoked. There were no photocopying machines, so we retyped paragraph after paragraph of boilerplate. If we made a mistake, we dabbed correction fluid on the first page and on all the carbon copies underneath it.

I was still the oddball in the group—a college kid, while the others never had the opportunity to go past high school. They would work until they married and had babies. I was Jewish, the others Sicilian. In my naïveté I had assumed they were all good little Catholic virgins, but when we sat around the cafeteria table at lunch, they told raunchy jokes and screamed with laughter. I grinned and blushed. Nobody I knew talked like that.

Fridays at noon, when we got our paychecks, we scorned the cafeteria and treated ourselves to lunch at a nearby Italian deli. I always ordered lasagna. They often ordered "gabagool" sandwiches, which I couldn't find on the menu. Later I learned it was the way they pronounced capicola. The girls watched their language in the deli—it was a tight-knit community, and the owners would know their families.

One of my coworkers, Theresa Taranto, took me under her wing. She showed me where to get materials from the supply cabinets and how to dial out on the extension phone. She had jet-black hair and creamy white skin—a high-energy gal, quick of speech and always in motion.

Whoever came up with the phrase "faster than a New York minute" must have been inspired by her.

I was enjoying this summer a lot more than the last. After a night at Louva's apartment, I'd go to work with her scent in my nostrils, and at each inhalation an exquisite current ran down to my groin. I'd call her during break, pretending I was chatting with my boyfriend "George." Maybe I should've been scared, but I don't remember that at all. By now I was used to keeping my sex life secret. My parents hadn't found out, and nothing bad had happened.

When we had coffee together Theresa confessed that she had a boyfriend. She'd gotten pregnant a couple of years ago. Her parents had sent her to a home for unwed mothers and made her give up the baby. Now she was dating a sailor who worked at the shipyard nearby. "I'm really worried," she confessed. "If I get pregnant again, my dad will kill me for sure."

"Birth control," I advised, and sent her to the Margaret Sanger Institute.

One day during break Theresa picked up the second extension. She hadn't noticed that I was already on the phone with "George." I saw her out of the corner of my eye—she heard Louva's voice and turned green as a hospital wall. Even before I hung up, she grabbed my elbow and was ushering me into the ladies' room. "Are you crazy?" she hissed. "You could get into so much trouble. If anyone finds out, you'll be fired."

I was astonished. Not only didn't she mind that I was gay, she was protecting me.

That summer we kept each other's secrets. We didn't stay in touch after I returned to school, but years later my father told me that Theresa was still working at the NRAO and sent her fondest regards.

11

A CULT IN THE CITY

My occasional nights with Louva continued in the same one-way pattern. She lay back and let me make love to her but didn't reciprocate. I thought she didn't find me attractive enough and kept hoping that would change. I did what I could to please her, including writing slushy poetry. Fortunately, none of that has survived. She kept encouraging me to leave my parents' home. By the end of the summer, I got up the nerve to take an apartment in Brooklyn, a short subway ride from my job at the Navy Regional Accounts Office. Louva never came to visit. Now that I was on my own and more available, she withdrew altogether.

I was alone, night after night, without a circle of supportive friends. Defeated, I quit the job and moved back home. For the next two months I slept most of the time, rising only to go to class.

Once I was back in my parents' home, Louva became more available. She let me make love to her once or twice and again urged me to leave home. She had started seeing a Sullivanian therapist named Ralph Klein and said I should get into therapy as well. I don't remember why I agreed to do so, but soon I was seeing Ann Keill.

The Sullivanians based their practice on a radical interpretation of the work of Harry Stack Sullivan, who theorized that interpersonal relationships and cultural forces were responsible for mental illness. Saul Newton, head of the Sullivan Institute, set up what was intended to be an alternative to the nuclear family. What it became was a cult.

Klein and Keill and the other Sullivanian therapists owned houses on the Upper West Side of Manhattan. They and their patients partied together and vacationed in the same part of the Hamptons. Patients were encouraged to leave their parents or divorce their spouses and socialize only within the group. We were urged to be nonmonogamous, which meant being sexually available to other group members. Former members report that Newton had female patients give him blow jobs. A current friend who knew Newton back then speaks of him with some admiration as a babe magnet. Another friend, rather less admiring, describes him as charismatic. These observations are confirmed in Amy B. Siskind's study of the community. My observation is that all cults function this way. They are deeply hierarchical, and money and sex flow upward to the Great Leader, the man at the top.

To me Newton was just an old guy I saw occasionally at parties. But then, I never found any man sexually irresistible, and what people consider charisma leaves me cold. I never idolized a political leader, rock star, or guru—I just don't respond to that energy.

The Sullivanians pressured gay patients to be bisexual. Dr. Keill told me that I was "cutting half the world out of my dating pool." This was considered very liberal, at a time when the psychiatric establishment labeled gay people as intrinsically disordered. At nineteen, I was too young and unsure of myself to reply that I didn't need a dating pool of three billion people. I did have brief affairs with a couple of men in the group—the gay ones, who were also trying to fit in. But I couldn't help noticing that heterosexuals were not pressured to be bisexual, and that Dr. Keill herself was married to a man, never showed up at Sullivanian parties, and apparently never slept with anyone other than her husband.

In the spring of 1963 I left home for good, on the day my mother rummaged through my dresser and found a diaphragm. She'd been searching my things and listening in on my phone calls with Patrick Fitzgerald, worrying that I would lose my virginity and not be able to marry a "nice Jewish boy." I'd lied to her when she found the birth control pills, saying I was holding them for a friend. But now I was

Me and one of the gay guys I dated during the Sullivanian years, dressed for an ACLU benefit. I felt like I was in drag.

done lying. I didn't tell her that I didn't need the diaphragm anymore because I'd broken up with Patrick and was having sex with a woman. Instead, I packed a bag and walked to the subway station.

I trudged up and down the side streets of northern Manhattan until I found a tiny room in a welfare hotel for $13.95 a week. It had a single bed and a sink. The bathroom was down the hall. Later I lugged in several boxes of books and stored them under the bed and tacked a Gauguin poster on the wall. I rode my bicycle down from the Bronx and chained it to the staircase railing in the lobby.

Food was another issue. I had always resisted my mother's attempts to teach me the housewifely arts. The only kitchen chore I had performed willingly was preparing chocolate pudding from a mix, with my sister's help. We took turns stirring and then got to lick the pot and spoon. During my short stay in the Brooklyn apartment, I had managed to rustle up meals, but that place had a stove and refrigerator. The welfare hotel, on the other hand, lacked a kitchen, and we weren't allowed to cook in our rooms. Since I couldn't afford to eat out all the time, I broke the rules and bought a hot plate and a small saucepan. On my first morning there I boiled an egg. Then I poured the water over a spoonful of instant coffee in my cup. It took me a long time to figure out why the coffee tasted so bad.

My net income from my part-time job was sixty dollars a week. Two sessions a week with Dr. Keill cost thirty dollars. When I asked why I should give her half my earnings, she said that our needs were different. She explained that she needed to own a house in the city and another in the Hamptons, in addition to supporting her two small children and paying for the nanny, while I needed to be in therapy, go to school, and work. To pay for the therapy, I ended up taking occasional babysitting and typing jobs on weekends.

Dr. Keill chain-smoked constantly. (She died of lung cancer in 1976.) Louva was another heavy smoker. Soon I had picked up the habit as well.

At the end of the spring semester, I took a full-time job and switched to full-time night school, attending four evenings a week. Weekends were for homework. That meant no time for judo, but I was determined to graduate as soon as possible rather than drag the BA out for a decade. I decided not to buy a TV—I couldn't afford the distraction.

Still in Sullivanian therapy, I began to attend Saturday night parties, and soon I had the social support that I had lacked in my first attempt to live on my own. During that period, I slept with a lot of men. Sometimes the sex was good, other times it was wretched, but love certainly had nothing to do with it.

Dr. Keill and one of her colleagues in the Sullivanian group did a bit of matchmaking and arranged for me to meet another college student my own age. Mike was also struggling with his feelings about being gay. I guess the idea was that we'd help each other to become straight, or at least bisexual.

The government was drafting young men to go and fight in Vietnam. At nineteen, Mike was subject to the draft after he graduated and his student deferment expired. Some men evaded conscription by fleeing across the border into Canada. Once they had done that, though, they couldn't come back—not without facing arrest. I offered to emigrate with him, but he said he planned to avoid combat duty by first continuing his studies in psychology and then joining the army as a psychologist. "In other words," I asked him, "you'll evaluate the draftees and decide which ones get sent to Vietnam to die?" After that conversation I lost a lot of respect for him.

A few years later, my cousin/brother Ira chose another method of avoiding going to war. By then the government had instituted a draft lottery, according to birth date. The 366 dates of the year were printed on slips of paper, and each slip was placed in an opaque plastic capsule. The capsules were mixed and poured into a deep glass jar. They were then drawn from the jar one at a time and opened. The first date picked was September 14, so all the men who shared that birthday were assigned lottery number 1 and were called up immediately. The lower the number, the sooner you would be called up. Ira got lottery number 4. When my father heard the news, he told me, "Vietnam never did anything to us. If Ira wants to go to Canada, I'll support him there."

However, Dad never made that offer clear to Ira, who enlisted in the air force instead, thinking that would keep him off the front lines. He was sent to Texas for basic training. As he tells it, he couldn't adjust. He couldn't even learn to march in step with the others. Ira has always marched to that different drummer. He was so miserable he sought help from an antiwar psychiatrist. His next step was to take a near-fatal overdose of pills, essentially a fake suicide attempt, after which he received a medical discharge.

I have to give the Sullivanians credit for some things. They encouraged me to leave home and to finish college, and they were against the Vietnam War from the get-go. In 1964, when the United States first became actively involved, I joined their contingent to march on the Pentagon. We held up a placard that read "C.I.A." in big letters, and in smaller print underneath, "Citizens In Action to end the war in Vietnam."

Although Dr. Keill exploited me financially, she actually seemed to like me and wanted me to do well. At one point she said she was experiencing countertransference and referred me to another therapist instead, Dr. Mildred Antonelli. Dr. Keill never told me what the issue was. Later, though, when I graduated from CCNY, both she and Dr. Antonelli came to the ceremony. They were obviously pleased with my success.

During the mid-1970s, long after I'd moved away from that insular society, the Sullivanians became increasingly authoritarian. According to a report in *Gothamist*, "Most members lived in sex-segregated apartments on the Upper West Side, where they were forbidden from engaging in exclusive relationships, unless approved by [Saul] Newton. Children born in the group were shipped off to boarding school or given to caretakers, with their parents only allowed to visit for an hour or two a day. In mandated weekly sessions, therapists advised patients to cut off all contact with outside friends and relatives, except when in need of money." The Sullivan Institute officially dissolved in 1991, when Newton died.

Gothamist points out that Newton was not formally trained as a clinician, but I don't see how training would have made a difference. The whole field is squirrelly. Until the gay liberation movement forced them to reconsider, psychologists who did have all the appropriate degrees considered homosexuality a mental illness and purported to cure it with aversion therapy, using mild electric shocks and induced vomiting. Psychiatrists subjected gay people to electroconvulsive "therapy." In earlier times, they had used castration or lobotomies.

In a more recent example of the less-than-scientific nature of the field (to put it kindly), psychologists James Mitchell and Bruce Jessen oversaw torture at Guantánamo, for which they received $180 million of our tax money.

12

ODD JOBS, ODD GIRLS

IN 1963, WHEN I LEFT HOME, my only skills were clerical. The companies that employed me now had invested in electric typewriters, faster and easier to work on than the manual ones the NRAO still used. I guess the government didn't see any need to improve our productivity, since it didn't have to make a profit. Copier machines had come on the market only recently, in 1961, so many offices didn't have them yet. They were enormous, heavy, and slow.

The want ads were still segregated by sex. The female section listed jobs for secretaries, typists, teachers, and nurses. You had to wear a dress or skirt and, for the interview only, a pair of little white gloves. After being hired you washed them and sent them back into hibernation in the dresser drawer.

I landed one tedious job after another, mostly working for grim older guys. The first was with a furniture company that seemed to be teetering on the edge of bankruptcy. When I'd completed the project they'd engaged me for, transferring files from handwritten cards to a more legible format, I was let go. The next was with the New York sales office of Levi Strauss, typing orders for jeans for three more grim guys. I talked them into hiring Louva, too, and we worked together until she was fired for absenteeism. Later I became so depressed in that environment that I started taking off one day a week, and then I was fired as well.

After that, I talked—or rather tested—my way into being secretary to the vice president of the Klein Institute for Aptitude Testing. I suppose they called themselves an institute to put on a veneer of scientific objectivity. They provided personality assessments of job applicants for other companies. Of course, anyone reasonably intelligent could figure out the correct answers. In most cases, you wanted to seem conservative and appropriately subservient. I showed up in a black suit and heels, filled in the right bubbles on the test form, and got the job. My boss was really a figurehead. I think his younger relatives managed the company. A crew of high school grads in the back room scored the tests. Bored witless, I snuck out of the VP office every chance I got and spent the time joking with the other kids—hey, I was only twenty myself! The kids had been taken in by my black suit and were surprised to discover that I wasn't another stuffed shirt. Soon enough, I was fired again.

The next job was as a circulation clerk with Hayden, a publisher of engineering magazines. The first time I saw the department manager, Nancy Merritt, in her office for the job interview, everything about her screamed "butch!" She wore no makeup, held a cigarette between her thumb and forefinger, and sat with her knees wide apart, spreading the skirt of what was maybe two steps above a housedress. I imagine she sized me up pretty quickly, too. The work consisted of filling out punch cards with information from people renewing their subscriptions. I don't know where the cards went—probably to a mainframe computer that collected the data, and then a printing system that spat out mailing labels for the magazines. Again, the work was painfully boring, but I was with other young people, and at least some of them were gay as well. Our boss evidently had a good eye. Four of us formed a little club, meeting after hours for a drink, gossip, and moral support. Occasionally I would write a humorous poem about the office and pass it around. Some of those verses found their way to Nancy's desk.

Nancy hired an assistant manager, Randall, who had recently graduated from some posh business school and was being trained to oversee us peons. In retrospect, I'm fairly sure he was as queer as the rest of us, but all we saw was an overprivileged kid. When he let it be known that he'd never seen a cockroach, a large one, recently deceased, appeared in an envelope on his desk. I must say he took it rather well.

I rarely saw Louva those days. Once in a while she would let me make love to her. More often she would tell me about her crush on some man, at one point her therapist, or at another time a guy who beat her, and how exciting that was. Needless to say, I found these confessions—or boasts—painful.

Louva changed jobs frequently, quitting or getting fired. Once she lost her apartment and asked to stay with me. She arrived that night with a boyfriend whose gestures seemed to indicate that he wanted a threesome. We all slept in my bed, the guy on one side, Louva in the middle, and me on the other side, furious. When she put her hand on me, I froze. They left in the morning.

A year or so later I encountered her on the street. She offered me the opportunity for one-way sex again. I walked off without a word. I never saw her again.

In June 1965 I got my diploma and said goodbye to Hayden. Nancy wrote me a little farewell poem, saying that I would be missed, ". . . not as a circulation clerk / but as a poet laureate." And then I was on my way to what I thought would be a professional career.

In 2003, wondering what had happened to Louva after all that time, I searched for her and learned that she'd had a career in documentary films and received quite a number of awards. However, she'd died very recently. In 2005, on a trip to New York with my wife, I went out to Brooklyn to meet Robert, a gay man who'd been Louva's best friend during the last years of her life. They had quite a bit in common, both coming from abusive families and having interests in metaphysics and astrology. They fought and made up many times. Robert learned to stop her when she transgressed his boundaries, and that was good for him. It must have been good for her to have a friend who didn't give up on her.

Robert told me that Louva had never quit smoking. She had no medical insurance, saw a psychic rather than a doctor, and collected information on arcane methods of healing from different cultures. Robert was into that as well. When Louva was dying—most likely from lung cancer—he even built her an orgone box, an expensive mid-twentieth-century piece of quackery that was supposed to cure all the ills of the body and of society.

Robert said that Louva should have been in galleries, that she was a talented artist but didn't know how to play the game. She would get into fights with people who could have helped her. He took photos of her art for a portfolio, but "she never pursued it." The paintings had vanished, except for one that he owned. I asked if I could see it. He showed me a small watercolor, a scattering of blue and pink splotches without a particular focus. I was surprised. I told Robert that I would have expected something as dramatic as Louva was, with big splashes of color and hard edges. "She expressed her softer side in the paintings," he replied.

What remains to me of that relationship? The knowledge of my passion for women. Memories bitter and sweet. And my name. Because of the slushy poetry I wrote to her, Louva gave me the nickname: Shelley, for the English Romantic poet. I forgot about it until 1967, when I joined the Daughters of Bilitis. The closeted lesbian running the New York chapter told me to use a pseudonym for the mailing list—which was postal, of course, long before e-mail lists—to avoid being persecuted by the FBI. I wrote Martha Shelley, c/o Martha Altman (my birth name), and then my address, thinking, *This is ridiculous. If the FBI wants to find me, they'll know where to look.* But in any case, that's who I became, first in our little lesbian society and then in the larger world: Martha Altman Shelley. It's on my passport.

13

WHAT HAPPENED
IN HARLEM

I GRADUATED FROM CITY COLLEGE of New York with a BA and the belief that it would lift me out of clerical jobs into a challenging intellectual career. However, it turned out that there were few positions open to someone without any specific skills, other than typing and the ability to read Chaucer in Middle English, and without connections such as a rich uncle willing to train me as a junior manager. The one option I found was to be a caseworker for the NYC Department of Welfare. All you needed was a bachelor's degree in any subject: ancient Greek literature, philosophy, zoology . . . it didn't matter. My pay jumped from $100 a week to around $120 a week.

New hires had three weeks of training in rules and procedures. First and most important, the instructor told us that we were now *profes-sionals*. We were going to be sent out into the community of welfare recipients to impose regulations on their disorderly lives and to teach them how to improve their lot in the future. Denying financial assistance was just as important as providing it, we were told, because it would help the clients become self-sufficient.

After those three weeks, I was assigned to visit indigent residents of an old-age home in the Bronx, one run by the Little Sisters of the Poor. Each person on my caseload of sixty had to be seen once a month, after which I filled out paperwork to let the department know that the individual was still alive and should continue to receive welfare checks.

I was twenty-one years old and bored silly, so I asked for a different assignment. You had to work in one location for six months before being allowed to transfer, unless you were willing to go to what was referred to as a "high crime area" like Bedford-Stuyvesant in Brooklyn, or Harlem. Since I now lived in Manhattan I chose Harlem, which is how I ended up in Unit 2 under the supervision of Mrs. Thelma Harrell, a kind and generous woman. We all adored her.

In those years the welfare centers were divided into units of five field caseworkers, each with a unit clerk and a supervisor. There was also one intake department with its own supervisor. The caseworkers where I was employed were almost exclusively White college graduates. The unit clerks were Black high school graduates. The supervisors and managers were also Black. Their civil service jobs would provide decent pay and benefits, as well as security and protection from the discrimination they faced in private industry. My cases were about half Black people and half Puerto Ricans, and all were single mothers.

I learned some important things on this job. One was that although clients received an automatic clothing grant, it was rarely enough for the family. Previous caseworkers, I was told, had insisted on inspecting these women's closets before writing up requisitions for additional grant money for clothes and bedding. When a client tried to show me what she had—or really, what she didn't have—I replied that she should just tell me what she needed. I would take the information back to Mrs. Harrell, who would OK the expenditure.

I already knew some Spanish. Because Francis Spellman, the Catholic cardinal, was enormously influential in New York politics, it was against the rules for the welfare caseworkers to give out information about contraception. Yet women were blamed for having children they couldn't support or for being deserted by the fathers. Some of us, of course, had no use for the cardinal, or for that rule, and ignored it. One of my coworkers carried fliers describing the various methods of birth control and gave them out to her clients. I learned the terms in Spanish—*la diafragma*, the diaphragm; *los pastellilos*, the pills—so I could discuss them with women who didn't speak English. I also referred people to the Margaret Sanger Institute, where I had first obtained these items for myself.

Most important, I learned that I was young and ignorant and in no position to teach a forty-year-old single mother of two, three, four, or eight how to manage on a welfare check that barely covered her rent.

Not wanting to be a caseworker forever, I applied and was accepted to the graduate English department at CCNY but had only the vaguest notion of what I would do with a master's degree in that subject. The first available night class was on the poetry of John Milton, a colossal bore and misogynist who seemed to think he was speaking for God. The dissonance between his words and what I saw every day in Harlem, what I heard every day about the Vietnam War, was unbearable. I stopped attending a few weeks into the semester.

I don't remember the names of any fellow caseworkers, except one: Allan Warshawsky, one of the kids from my junior high school class. He remembered me from junior high as well, when we encountered each other in Harlem. A few of us put together a newsletter, which we called *Harlem River Trane*, after jazz great John Coltrane. It was leftish, pro-worker. I wrote under the pseudonym Sergei—it didn't take Allan long to figure out who "Sir Gay" was. (We ran into each other yet again, four years later, in the Gay Liberation Front.) I also drew cartoons satirizing the Welfare Department and posted them on the square pillars that supported the center's high ceiling.

In July 1967, we caseworkers went on strike.

The NYC Department of Welfare had seen a massive strike in February 1965, four months before I was hired. Everyone—caseworkers, clerks, supervisors—had participated. They had won significant pay raises, health insurance, a reduction in case size from over 120 to a maximum of 60, and an automatic clothing grant for clients.

By 1967, though, the case size was creeping up again. Union organizers called meetings at every center and gave us pep talks. We had a citywide meeting in a larger auditorium. The *New York Times* covered it with a snarky article in which we were all described as wearing "beards and miniskirts." In other words, we were to be dismissed as a bunch of hippies. I don't think the *Times* ever supported a strike in its entire history, except maybe one directed against a Communist government.

I am generally a soft-spoken person, but while leading chants on the picket line, I learned that I could shout loud enough to be heard down the block. As a protest, and at the request of the union, I also slept several nights on an air mattress in front of City Hall. By morning the air had leaked out and I was sleeping on the hard sidewalk, in need of a bath and change of clothes. Neither the mayor's office nor the news media noticed me.

The strike was a bust. Unlike the one in 1965, only caseworkers went out. We didn't attempt to pull in the clerks (who by now had a separate union), probably because we'd bought into the notion that, unlike those mere high school graduates, we were "professionals." Our implicit racism and intellectual snobbery defeated us. During the strike, the clerks and supervisors kept the welfare centers running. It didn't take long for the city to decide there was no need to come to terms with us. The new contract had no maximum limit on case size. Other terms were unfavorable as well.

My sister, Jeannette, had a somewhat different experience. She worked for the department from 1969 to 1971, while attending law school at night. The strikes were history by then. Her supervisors and other caseworker friends in the Bronx were Black. When she transferred to Brooklyn, both her supervisor and all the caseworkers were White.

By the time the strike was over and I returned to work, the Harlem Welfare Center management had figured out that Unit 2 was giving out more clothing grant money than any other in the center, and they broke us up. I don't know where they sent Mrs. Harrell. I also don't remember my new supervisor's name, but he was one of those I-pulled-myself-up-by-my-bootstraps-why-can't-you? types, with a sour disposition, so I thought of him as Mr. Peptic Ulcer. I couldn't stand him and asked to be transferred to Intake.

Intake work consisted of interviewing applicants and either accepting or rejecting them. Most I accepted: The carpenter who'd come up from the South, found work, and was laid off shortly afterward. The woman whose new baby was born brain damaged. Heroin addicts just discharged from rehab. The addicts came to us in droves, because the Mafia was pushing heroin hard in Black communities. We opened their cases, gave them a first check, and generally never saw them again—they used the money from that first check to shoot up. I did turn down one guy who'd managed to get his fix between the time the rehab center discharged him and the time he showed up at my desk, already nodding out.

On Thursday night, April 4, 1968, Martin Luther King was murdered, and with him the hopes of many Black Americans for peaceful progress. The next morning, instead of taking the bus, I climbed into a sedan jammed with ten other White caseworkers. We kept our heads below the car windows so as not to present a target, peeking up now and then at burnt-out stores, at pavement glittering with broken glass. When we arrived at work, we found that everyone, including clerks and supervisors, had been told to crouch when walking past windows, some of which already had bullet holes. I heard a couple of shots during the day.

Official labor statistics show very low unemployment rates from 1965 to 1970, perhaps because so many young men had been drafted and were no longer counted as out of work. Yet the reverse seemed to be happening in the communities that we served. More and more Black people had lost their jobs, and they flooded the welfare centers. The intake staff couldn't handle them all. One afternoon a father of five, who'd been sent from a Brooklyn office the day before and waited all day in Harlem, only to be turned away again, yanked a water fountain out of the wall, overturned rows of chairs, and then picked one chair up and hurled it through the supervisor's window. *Good going, man!* I thought. Fortunately, he left before anyone could call the cops.

Another day a young couple came in, having left their children with relatives. The man explained that he'd been laid off and survived the week by borrowing five dollars from one friend and five dollars from another. I took his file to Mr. G, the intake supervisor, for approval. He told me to have the applicant go back to his friends and ask each for a note verifying the loan. I said I would not humiliate the man that way. I dropped the file on Mr. G's desk, explained to the young couple what had happened, and walked off the job.

14

A SALUTE TO THE PIONEERS

IN 1967, WHEN I JOINED the Daughters of Bilitis (DOB), I was twenty-three and knew very little about gay American history. Over the years I've learned more about what those who came before me accomplished.

During the McCarthy era, the late 1940s through 1950s, it was truly dangerous to be gay. We were arrested, imprisoned, beaten, fired from our jobs, and subjected to electroshock therapy. We were systematically hunted out of federal employment and military service. During this period, notorious for persecution of anyone tainted with the slightest suspicion of Communist connection, more suspected gays were expelled from the government than suspected Communists.

Only a handful of gay men and lesbians were willing to be out in those early years. Those brave individuals founded the Mattachine Society, for gay men, in Los Angeles in 1950 and the lesbian organization, the Daughters of Bilitis (DOB), in San Francisco in 1955.

Those groups, and others that arrived a bit later, worked hard to present us as respectable citizens and plead, politely, for acceptance into mainstream America. Tactics included writing letters and communicating with clergy and politicians. They used the word *homophile* instead of *homosexual* because they didn't want straight people to think about us having S-E-X. They would have considered the word *gay* inappropriate, likely for the same reason, but also because liberal newspapers like the *Village Voice* and *New York Times* wouldn't print it.

From 1959 to 1969 the homophile organizations demonstrated against police harassment, against firing gay employees, and, in 1966, against a New York State law banning known homosexuals from being served liquor. Some of these activities were successful, in a limited way. The New York State Liquor Authority didn't change its rules, but the city's human rights commission did come out against the discrimination.

Then came the '60s, with an acceleration of the civil rights movement, the rebirth of feminism, a loosening of sexual mores, antiwar activities, and a cultural revolution that expressed itself in art, music, apparel, and psychedelic drugs. The traditional homophile groups were careful to avoid any identification with those movements, except that in the DOB, there were nods to feminism. Hoping not to offend any of the mainstream constituencies whose approval they sought, they distanced themselves from other social justice issues, limiting themselves to simply begging for inclusion into the existing social order.

Perhaps their most militant display took place on May 21, 1966—a fifteen-car motorcade in Los Angeles demanding admission of gays into the armed forces. That same day, smaller contingents also marched and picketed for the cause in Philadelphia, San Francisco, and Washington, DC. In recent years, some have dubbed the motorcade "the first gay pride parade."

This action came at a time when President Johnson was escalating the Vietnam War—and when tens of thousands of Americans, including me, were in the streets demonstrating against it. I understand that the point of the motorcade was to protest our exclusion from military service and the persecution of those who had signed up and were later discovered to be gay. But that the largest public action the existing gay organizations ever put on consisted of pleading for our right to enlist in a genocidal war—a war that killed over two million Indo-Chinese people who had never done anything to the United States—made me sick to my stomach. And still does.

Even so, I have to give the organizations credit. In the long run, despite their limitations, the Mattachine Society and the Daughters of Bilitis were the womb that birthed the Gay Liberation Front.

15

FROM THE BARS
TO BARNARD

ONCE MY RELATIONSHIP WITH LOUVA WAS OVER, I started looking for other women like me. I'd heard that lesbian bars existed, but since gay relationships were outlawed, the bars kept a very low profile. Many had no signs over the doors, and the windows were covered so no one could see inside. I found one such place in Greenwich Village and tried looking for love there, but I struck out time and time again. In the bar culture you had to identify as either butch or femme, wearing men's trousers with a shirt and tie, or a tight dress, nylons, and lipstick. I would show up in a pair of jeans and a plaid shirt. People like me were called *ki-ki* (rhymes with *bye-bye*) and were not welcome.

The bars never became a social or political home for me. My worst experience in one of those Mafia-run establishments was on a night when I sat at the counter, inhaling the scents of spilled beer, cigarette smoke, and some drugstore perfume that I couldn't identify, and trying to make small talk with the woman on my right. Another woman took the stool to my left and the two of them—who obviously knew each other—began to sing "Deutschland über Alles," a song closely identified with the Nazis' regime. I didn't actually know whether these women were German, but it was clear that they had spotted me as a Jew and were letting me know what they thought of our kind. I left immediately. It was a long time before I could bring myself to enter a bar again.

In November 1967, when I was twenty-three, I found my way to a Daughters of Bilitis meeting. The DOB rented a suite in an office building, inexpensive but in a reasonably safe area, with nondescript furniture and no decorations on the walls. Like the bars, we kept a low profile.

Our DOB chapter had monthly business meetings during which we folded and addressed the newsletter. It included a calendar of events: a dance, a lecture by a psychologist telling us why we gays weren't crazy, or an evening with a middle-aged lesbian couple who lived in suburban New Jersey and would give us tips on how to make our relationship work. There were about two hundred women on the mailing list, though only a handful showed up for events.

Jean Powers and Eleanor Kravitz, the couple who ran the New York chapter, were in their early forties, both tall and stout. Jean always attended meetings, but Eleanor rarely came to the office, and I never got to know her particularly well. She was Jewish, worked as a bookkeeper, and was disabled from having survived polio.

Jean was from Oklahoma. She once told me that she was eligible to join the Daughters of the American Revolution, but I doubt she would have fit in. She'd been forced out of the Defense Department, suspected of being gay, and in any case was too big, too smart, and too well organized—qualities that would get a man promoted to manager, but that men found threatening in a woman. She used her managerial skills to keep our chapter running, and during the day she had some kind of computer job. Despite our differences—she was a Republican and I was far to the left of Democrat—we seemed to like each other.

Jean and Eleanor saw that they could make use of my youth and enthusiasm, and they asked me to run for treasurer. I was honored until I realized that I was recruited because no one else wanted the job. I recorded income and expenditures in a black composition notebook, including the times when I borrowed fifteen cents for carfare and reimbursed the treasury when I got my paycheck.

After two months Eleanor reviewed my work. "These are the screwiest books I've ever seen," she said. "It took me a week to make head or tail of them. But I'll give you this: you didn't steal a penny."

"Nobody ever taught me how to keep books," I replied.

Eleanor took the job back. She and Jean then tried me out as chapter president. That didn't work well either. I had no idea what the duties were, and they hadn't given me a to-do list. Finally, since I was a frequent and articulate participant in our group discussions, they asked me to be the public speaker. That meant being out, being publicly known as gay. Perhaps because McCarthyism had been discredited, perhaps because I hadn't invested years in a career that could be destroyed if I were known to be gay, perhaps because I was young and immortal, I said yes.

My first assignment as spokeswoman came when the professor of an abnormal psychology class at a local college requested that we send a representative. I used what I'd learned in statistics, explaining that "normal" just means you're in the middle of a bell curve, or in the majority. It's normal to be right-handed. In America, it's normal to be White. So the first thing I did when addressing the class was to remind them of that definition. Next, I'd pass out little slips of paper and ask the students to make an X if they were attracted to their own sex, a Y if attracted to the opposite, and XY if attracted to both. "Don't let anyone else see what you wrote. Fold the papers and then pass them to me." As usual, out of thirty students, three or four indicated they were gay or bisexual. I'd announce the results, knowing that the straight students would be wondering who among them was gay, and the gays would be feeling less alone.

One evening in the spring of 1968 I went to a DOB party and, after a few drinks and turns around the floor, went home with my dance partner. She was in the kitchen making coffee when I awoke, a little fuzzy but still in post-climactic bliss. *I think she said her name was Allison.* As it turned out I'd remembered correctly, despite those extra beers.

My pick-up date—my new lover—lived in Englewood, New Jersey, about a twenty-minute drive from the Upper West Side apartment I shared with a friend. That was the beginning of a passionate summer for us.

Allison Jennings was Irish, with red hair, and was employed as a tech writer. She was forty-one but told me she was thirty-nine, so as not to scare a twenty-four-year-old off. (I wouldn't have cared.) What I also didn't know was that she and Jean Powers had been lovers for many years, and I never did find out why they broke up. They were still good friends. Allison was from Toledo, had voted for Goldwater in 1964 and, like Jean, had worked for the Defense Department—specifically, for the nuclear program. Unlike Jean, she hadn't been forced out. One day she came across a document that referred to "megadeaths." She asked her supervisor if that word meant what it sounded like. He said yes. As soon as she found another job in the civilian sector she resigned.

It was a decade of high-profile assassinations: JFK in 1963 and Malcolm X in 1965, MLK in April 1968 and RFK in June 1968. The Vietnam War raged on. Then summer came.

On July 4, 1968, a handful of gay men and women rode the bus to Philadelphia for the annual Day of Remembrance. Barbara Gittings, who had founded the New York DOB chapter but was no longer a member, had organized the first of these pickets in 1965, along with Frank Kameny of the Mattachine Society. I was the only current member of New York DOB who showed up that year. We picketed in front of Independence Hall and held up placards protesting discrimination against homosexuals. We were expected to look respectable. The men were required to wear jackets and ties, the women skirts or dresses, heels, and pantyhose. It may have been a positive experience for some, but I hated it, hated having to wear a dress and pretend to be "normal," hated the tourists who stared at us as though we were zoo animals or carnival freaks.

In August, at the Democratic National Convention in Chicago, antiwar and antiestablishment protesters were met with a police riot. The police clubbed and tear-gassed indiscriminately, assaulting peaceful demonstrators, onlookers, and residents of the neighborhood. Allison and I followed the reports and were infuriated. She already had ceased voting Republican, but the Democrats didn't give us much of an alternative.

The Democratic honchos chose Vice President Hubert Humphrey. He was called a "liberal" but had committed to carry on President Johnson's war. He hadn't competed in any of the primaries. Humphrey was a nebbish, a party hack without an appealing platform. The inner-city riots after MLK was assassinated, antiwar demonstrations on college campuses, and the police riot in Chicago frightened many Americans—particularly Whites and older voters. Richard Nixon, Humphrey's opponent, declared himself the law-and-order candidate who could end the tumult and who also had a "secret plan" to end the Vietnam War. He got a plurality of the popular vote—segregationist George Wallace peeled off 13.5 percent—but an overwhelming majority in the Electoral College.

I'd been on many antiwar demonstrations and didn't believe a word either candidate said. Nixon's victory only reinforced my determination to speak out against injustice, whether the victims were Vietnamese peasants—or people like me.

In August 1968 I had quit the Welfare Department, but I still needed to pay the rent. The liberal arts BA that I had worked so hard for didn't lead to a professional career, but I could always fall back on my clerical skills. The employment agency found me a secretarial job at Barnard College.

I had no idea what I was getting into.

16

THE CLOSETS
OF ACADEME

My boss was Jean T. Palmer, the general secretary of the college, which meant she oversaw everything nonacademic, including fundraising and admissions. I would be her secretary. I saw her as a nice lady from the Midwest, probably upper middle class, warm, and well mannered. She was short like I was, but with white hair and sparkling blue eyes. She was just about to turn sixty-five and would retire at the end of the academic year. I don't know how she saw me.

I shared an office with Rebecca, the bookkeeper, who was the only Black woman that I noticed among the administrative or clerical staff. A hard worker, she once let me know that I was paid more than she was just because I had that BA, and I had to agree with her. Typing wasn't more valuable than bookkeeping. No doubt race played a role.

At the time I let my hair grow down below my shoulders, and we all had to wear skirts to work. But in the evening I switched to jeans and hung out with my lover Allison or went to Daughters of Bilitis meetings. Although I was out as spokesperson for the DOB, I couldn't be out at work. I was still living a double life.

Barnard was the sister school to all-male Columbia University across the street, where student Bob Martin had founded the first Student Homophile League (using the alias Stephen Donaldson). I don't remember how we first met, but it may have been when I joined his group to take part in an antiwar demonstration on campus. Naturally, in the fall of 1968, some of the straight protesters were uncomfortable with our openly gay presence.

Bob was bisexual, and at that time I was still under the sway of Sullivanian therapists who had urged me to have relationships with both sexes. We started an affair. Since we were both speakers for gay organizations, this annoyed the older leaders in the homophile movement—and to tell the truth, we enjoyed annoying them. They put up with us, though, because it was hard to find people who were willing to be publicly identified as gay. Perhaps, also, because we were just kids. I was twenty-four, and he was twenty-two.

One day Bob introduced me to LSD, guiding my adventure with music and, later that afternoon, taking me to the movies to see *2001: A Space Odyssey*. We sat in the front row with all the other tripped-out hippies watching the light show. Dr. Keill, my therapist, had once warned me against the drug, saying it was like driving 90 mph blindfolded, but instead of crashing, I had a fantastic time—one of many experiences that drew me away from the Sullivanian influence. A few days later I taped a second poster over my desk: the first was of Martin Luther King, the new one a psychedelic illustration of the Beatles' song, "Lucy in the Sky with Diamonds."

My next assignment as DOB spokeswoman was an interview with a reporter for WOR radio, which was doing a show on the "sexual revolution." It was to be aired the following day. I disliked the reporter and went home with a headache. The next morning I was sitting at my desk when Miss Palmer sailed in. "Guess what!" she said. "WOR radio was here last night, interviewing girls from the new coed dormitory, and I must stay up tonight and tune in."

In a panic, I called Jean Powers. "What am I going to do? The boss is going to hear my voice on that program."

"Just call the radio station and explain," Jean replied calmly. "They'll understand, and they'll take that segment off the air."

I couldn't do it. Maybe it was the poster of Martin Luther King looking down at me. Maybe it was the question I'd always asked myself—what would you do if you'd been a German under the Nazi regime? Would you have been too cowardly to stand up for the persecuted, or brave enough to resist the regime? During the rest of the workday I was so obviously agitated that my coworkers wondered aloud what was wrong with me, though they didn't ask directly.

At 5:00 PM, just as the boss was about to leave, I gathered my courage. "Miss Palmer," I said, "I'm going to be on that WOR radio program."

"What for?"

"I'm representing the Daughters of Bilitis."

"What's that?"

"A civil rights organization." I started to sweat. "For lesbians."

Miss Palmer gave me a big wink. "How nice that you young people are involved in so many causes! Now help me on with my coat, dear. I'm going to be late for the opera."

I knew nothing about Barnard's history and internal politics when I fell into a secretarial job there—but over that one academic year, I learned plenty. The one thing I'd guessed correctly about Miss Palmer was that she hailed from the Midwest—she was from Omaha. During the next few months of 1968, after she'd come out to me with that big wink, she let me know a bit more about her life.

Miss Palmer had been head of the WAVES (the women's branch of the US Naval Reserves) before coming to Barnard, and she had been the leading force in getting the US Navy to let women become "yeomen." These women were often well educated, trained as what we would now call executive assistants, but without the yeoman classification, they couldn't receive the same pay as men who did the same job but who also held the title. This was a big step up for them, since during the 1940s women in the civilian world generally got a little over half a man's wages. The sailors weren't pleased, though, because when women took over the military's clerical jobs, the men who would have been doing them were released for combat.

Now and again, Miss Palmer let me know that some of the women who ran Barnard were lesbians. Among them was Virginia Gildersleeve, who'd been the dean of the college from 1911 to 1946. In 1952 the title was changed from "dean" to "president." Martha Peterson, the president at the time I worked there, was one of us as well.

Miss Palmer's tone of voice conveyed quite a bit of admiration for Gildersleeve. She always let me know what she thought about people. For example, Eleanor Elliott, an alumna and trustee, was one of the principal fundraisers. Since the general secretary oversaw fundraising, Mrs. Elliot spent quite bit of time in our office.

One day Miss Palmer asked me what I thought of Elliott. "She seems OK," I replied cautiously. I really didn't know much about her, except that she appeared to be in her early forties, stylish, and very upper middle class. She smiled, but almost never spoke to me.

"She's a snob," Miss Palmer said flatly.

———————

The employment agency had charged me $300 for sending me to Barnard. The college promised that if I lasted six months, I'd get a refund of the $300 and a week's paid vacation.

In February 1969, at the end of my initial six months, I received the $300 and my week off. I called Rita LaPorte, the national president of Daughters of Bilitis, who agreed to let me stay in her home in San Francisco.

When I left Manhattan there was snow on the ground. When I arrived in San Francisco, blossoming plum trees scented the air. I'd grown up in neighborhoods of brownstone and brick, of a steady rain of soot that grayed the building facades and grimed their residents' faces and clothes. In San Francisco the hills were dotted with Victorian houses painted in three or more colors: white and pale blue, with indigo accents; white and light tan, with crimson trim. . . . Who would dare paint a New York City building white?

Rita told me she'd been in the military, but her experience was quite different from Miss Palmer's. Like so many other enlisted women, she'd been raped, and the pain and anger were still with her. I also met Del Martin and Phyllis Lyon, two of the organization's founders, in a little café. Unlike Rita, they seemed quite cheerful.

I took a day to visit Berkeley. On a stroll through the UC campus I got caught up in a student antiwar demonstration but wasn't arrested. Lunch was at a vegetarian restaurant: avocado, tomato, and sprouts on fresh-baked, whole-grain bread. I never ate avocados in New York—they were prohibitively expensive. My only previous taste of the fruit had been in fourth grade, when our teacher cut one up and gave each student a tiny square. In California you could slather avocados on your sandwich or dump chunks in your salad.

I'm going to move here, I told myself.

Upon returning to New York I was given a new assignment: to represent DOB in a series of debates on morning TV. My opponents were psychiatrist Charles Socarides and psychoanalyst Irving Bieber. They both believed homosexuality was an illness and could be cured. It seems that they made a good living tormenting gay people by providing an early form of conversion therapy. I despised them.

Once the series had been taped, I decided that I had better come out to my mother before she heard about it from one of my aunts, who might catch the show. I had already told my father. I thought he'd be shocked. Instead, I was. "So what else is new?" he said. "I knew that already from your drawings and poetry. Don't tell your mother. She'll blame me."

Predictably enough, Mom didn't take it well. She blamed Dad for not disciplining me enough and my popular kid sister for not getting me dates with boys. She offered to spend the money she'd been saving for my wedding on a psychiatric cure, or on a plastic surgeon who would amputate a chunk of my Semitic nose to make me more attractive to men. I turned down both offers.

During my lunch breaks, I started going to meetings really intended for the students. At one I met famed anthropologist Margaret Mead, another alumna of the college. She was sixty-seven at the time and rather disabled, with a bandaged knee. I remember her complaining that young people don't listen to their elders anymore.

"That's because our elders are sending our brothers to die in Vietnam," I retorted. She didn't respond. Later I learned from another anthropologist that Mead was privately opposed to the war, but she never spoke out publicly against it.

Another meeting I attended presented a rosy picture of the prospects new graduates would enjoy. I spoke up again, to the effect that my own bachelor's degree hadn't opened many doors. At the time I didn't have the facts to confirm my assertion that an Ivy League diploma wouldn't get female students much further than one from CCNY. Last year, though, alumna Elisheva Yuval wrote me that when she matriculated in 1961, then president Millicent McIntosh addressed the incoming freshmen: "Here at Barnard you will receive the best education available to women anywhere in the world. But if you want to get a job after graduation, learn to type."

By the time I returned to my desk, someone had already notified Miss Palmer of my speaking up. "Academic freedom is only for faculty and students," she warned me. "It doesn't apply to administrative staff."

My subversive behavior must have come to the attention of one faculty member, Kate Millett. She sought me out and we met a couple of times, and then in December she told me she'd been fired, at least in part due to her support of student antiwar protests, despite being popular with the students. I asked if she wanted me to help organize a demonstration on her behalf. She declined, saying that she preferred to spend her energies finishing a book she was working on. That book turned out to be the bestseller *Sexual Politics*.

Jean Palmer retired at the end of the spring semester. I was offered a contract for a second year at Barnard, working for whoever would replace her. I turned them down, remembering Miss Palmer's admonition:

academic freedom, the freedom to speak one's mind, doesn't apply to administrative staff. Instead, I moved to the Lower East Side, to a cheap apartment and a three-day-a-week job that would allow time for writing and political organizing.

17

THE NIGHT WE SET
ON FIRE

BY THE TIME I LEFT BARNARD, at the beginning of June 1969, I already had a new job lined up.

I had previously done a few weekend typing gigs for a woman named Virginia Admiral. Her shop, Academy Typing and Typesetting, occupied a loft in Greenwich Village. Hers was the kind of small business where the work takes place in front, and the owner lives in the back. As I remember, the front room had ten stations, some with electric typewriters, others with new machines that did cold-type composition. These resembled typewriters but had little balls for different fonts and could justify the copy. You loaded them with sheets of shiny white paper. Two additional stations had light boxes for cutting and pasting the output, along with any photos. Once the pages were composed, they could be taken to the printer. This is how books, pamphlets, and newspapers were produced before computers.

Virginia was fifty-four, with white hair and pale blue eyes behind thick glasses, and smoked little cigars. She frequently rode her bicycle around the Village to pick up and deliver work. She was also involved in the antiwar movement and the local arts community, and was quite an artist herself. Her son—a kid my own age named Robert de Niro—was an aspiring actor, and she'd been his sole support for years, while his father made a career as an abstract expressionist painter. She agreed to take me on for three days a week at three dollars an hour, and set me to work on one of the cold-type machines.

Virginia was one of the many great bosses I've worked for. She did have her quirks. If she was in a bad mood, usually because clients hadn't paid on time, she would complain that I made too many mistakes. "So fire me," I'd reply calmly. She would huff a bit and walk out of the room.

Gilbert Burgos, one of my coworkers, took me under his wing, helping me when I had trouble with some of the equipment. He was a big, boisterous guy. Sometimes we got together after hours, along with his wife Faye, to enjoy a couple of beers and a puff of weed. Gil would make a joke and then howl with laughter at it. One day he introduced me to another friend, Jonathan Ned Katz, who subsequently became a noted historian of gay life. Although I lost contact with Gil and Faye, I stayed in touch with Jonathan. Recently he told me he remembered that occasion very well, that I was one of the first out gay people he met, saying "look where you led me. Pretty good!"

Years later, after de Niro became successful and Virginia retired, I stopped by to visit her. During our conversation, she asked, "All my other employees resented me—why didn't you? After all, you were my wage slave."

"I only worked three days a week," I replied. "The rest of the time I was free to run around and raise hell."

She sighed and said that she'd been the one in shackles—to the business and to single parenthood, 24/7.

———————

After Virginia hired me, I found a place I could afford on part-time wages—a third-floor walk-up for sixty dollars a month, about a mile and a half east of the new job.

Manhattan's Lower East Side was a neighborhood of decaying tenements. They'd been built in the mid- to late 1800s to accommodate a growing population and then became home to the usual waves of immigrants. First came the Germans, next the Irish, and around the turn of the twentieth century, Jews, Italians, Greeks, and Eastern Europeans. New arrivals worked in the garment industry until they or their descendants prospered and moved out to more comfortable quarters of the city. By the late 1960s the neighborhood was a mix of working class or impoverished Puerto Ricans, Black people, and some White immigrants, as well as young people of various ethnicities who, like myself, had chosen to live in a low-rent area in order support their dreams as artists, musicians, hippies, and political activists. (As the area became gentrified, people started to call that section the East Village.)

The bedroom window of my new abode opened to an air shaft. There was a shower, but the toilet was down the hall and shared with other tenants on the floor. If you left your toilet paper there, it would get stolen, so you kept it in your apartment and carried it with you as the necessity arose. I hauled up the bit of furniture I'd managed to accumulate over the years. One sunny day, while walking around the neighborhood, I scored a prize: someone had abandoned a large wooden desk on the sidewalk, a plain, sturdy item that had likely belonged to a now-defunct business. I claimed it by sitting on it until a friend happened by who could help me carry it home. That was decades before cell phones.

A few days later Mom came to visit. She grew very distressed when I showed off my acquisition. Here I was living in the neighborhood she had struggled to escape, during the years when she sewed in the garment factories. And scavenging furniture! As a child in Havana, she had felt humiliated when Grandpa brought home a used dresser he found in the street. She was so proud that she could go to Macy's now and order a brand-new living room set.

Jean Powers phoned me during the last week of June. Two women visiting from Boston wanted to start a DOB chapter there. They were staying at Jean and Eleanor's apartment. Would I be willing to give them a tour of Greenwich Village on Saturday night? Of course, I said. I called Allison, my lover at the time, and told her I'd come to her place after escorting the Boston ladies around town.

Saturday, June 28, 1969, was a typically hot summer day in the city. It had reached ninety-two degrees at midday, and even after dinner, when I picked up the visitors, the temperature still hovered around ninety. One of the women hardly said a word, and I don't remember her name. The other, Pat Peterson, was tall, athletic, and full of funny stories. She'd been born in the South and raised Baptist. At adolescence she started having sexual feelings for other women. Like other lesbians I've met, she thought she could squelch these troubling feelings by converting to Catholicism and entering a very strict order. Since she is naturally about as diffident as a locomotive, she managed to convince whoever was in charge that she had a real calling and was accepted into a Franciscan convent.

The mother superior picked her up at the train station and drove her to the monastery. When they passed through the gate, Pat nodded toward the statue of a man with a tonsure haircut and asked cheerfully, "Who's the guy with the birds?"

Mother Superior glanced up at St. Francis, then at the new postulant in the passenger seat, and replied quietly, "My dear, you have a lot to learn."

As one might expect, being confined with scores of other young women did nothing to subdue Pat's lesbian tendencies—nor was her personality suited to convent life. One day the novices were asked to collect windfalls from under the apple tree. Noticing that the branches were still full, Pat climbed the tree and began tossing the fruits into the other novices' aprons. "It was like shooting baskets," she recounted. Then one girl started waving frantically and pointing. Pat turned around. Mother Superior had come down from the house and looked furious.

Pat soon left the order and moved north. Now she was going to bring the same energy and enthusiasm to another all-female organization, the Daughters of Bilitis.

I don't remember any of the watering holes or landmarks we visited, except one: we were walking along Christopher Street when we came upon a group of young men throwing things at cops. The visitors were startled. "What's going on?" Pat exclaimed.

"It's just a riot," I replied, assuming that we'd encountered yet another antiwar demonstration. "We have them all the time." Since I didn't patronize gay men's bars, I wasn't aware that we were passing the Stonewall Inn, or that such a place even existed.

As we subsequently learned, the rioters were young gay men and one butch lesbian responding to a police raid. Some of the males were drag queens. (As far as I know, none of them called themselves transsexuals in those days, instead using the term *transvestites*, though a few may have adopted that label or actually transitioned in later years.) The Stonewall, like similar establishments, was Mafia-owned and paid protection money to the police department. But this was an election year, and the cops had been ordered to "clean up the city." That meant rounding up prostitutes in Times Square and raiding the gay bars. Usually the gays made no resistance, instead covering their faces as they were herded into paddy wagons.

This time was different. The gays threw things at cops, even locking some of them into the bar and trying (unsuccessfully) to set the place on fire. Rioting went on for several nights.

That Saturday night, though, I had no idea that we were witnessing an event of enormous significance. We turned aside to avoid the fray. I led my Boston charges to the nearest subway entrance and delivered them to Jean and Eleanor's place.

From there I took the subway north to the 181st Street station, expecting to catch the bus to Englewood, New Jersey, where Allison lived. But it was around 3:00 AM, and the buses had stopped running. I decided to walk across the George Washington Bridge. It was very quiet and still hot. The full moon hung like a brass shield in a pitch-black sky—you can't see stars in NYC—somewhat to the southwest and directly over the equally pitch-black Hudson River, a silent, immense python slithering toward the sea.

Once on the Jersey side, I stuck my thumb out. A medical resident just getting off his shift picked me up and drove me to Englewood.

Sunday afternoon Allison and I attended a DOB discussion group, but there was no mention of the rioting in Greenwich Village. I'm sure no one present had heard about it.

Monday—another hot, sticky summer day—found me lazing around, trying to recover from a weekend of too little sleep, when I saw the story in the *New York Times*: "Heavy police reinforcements cleared the Sheridan Square area of Greenwich Village again yesterday morning when large crowds of young men, angered by a police raid on an inn frequented by homosexuals, swept through the area . . ."

I jumped up immediately, on fire, thinking, *This is our moment*, and phoned Jean Powers. "We gotta have a protest march!"

"Why don't you call Mattachine?" she replied. "If the guys want to do it, we can jointly sponsor a march."

18

"WE WILL BE BACK!"

AFTER HANGING UP FROM THE CONVERSATION WITH JEAN POWERS, I called Dick Leitsch, head of the Mattachine Society. He didn't seem particularly enthusiastic. He did tell me that his organization was having a meeting at a public auditorium downtown and said I could attend and make my proposal.

When I arrived, the hall was packed: four hundred gay guys, one female Mattachine member, and me. I found myself sitting next to a fortyish guy named Bob Kohler. He spoke passionately about young gays in the streets, some still in their teens, thrown out by their parents for being homosexual. Having no job skills, they earned their living by prostitution and desperately needed help.

When I had my turn to speak and suggested a protest march, Leitsch asked how many people were in favor of it. A forest of hands went up. I think that surprised him, because he was used to being the only public spokesman for gays in the city—everyone else was cowering in the closet. At the end of the meeting, he said that those who wanted to organize it should meet "over in that corner."

We formed a committee on the spot and agreed to meet the following Saturday at the Mattachine offices. I am fairly sure I was the only woman present. There were eight guys or so, including Bob Kohler and another man, Marty Robinson. It was a hot afternoon, and we were drinking cold beers and in high spirits—actually, a little tipsy. At one point someone uttered the words, "Gay Liberation Front."

I whacked the table a couple of times and hollered, "That's it! That's it! We're the Gay Liberation Front!" Then I noticed blood running down my palm. I had been slamming my hand against a pop-top from a beer can—but with the beer and the excitement, I was feeling no pain.

Leitsch, who'd been doing something with a mimeo machine in the adjoining room, rushed in. Were we starting a new gay organization right here in his own offices, one that would take members away from Mattachine?

"Oh, no," I lied, "of course not, that's just the name of our march committee." Did he believe me, even for a second? I don't know.

We decided on Sunday, July 27, exactly one month after the riots. Mattachine and DOB took out an ad in the *Village Voice* advertising the event. The ad appeared on Thursday, July 24. My job was to ask the police about permits. I was understandably nervous about talking to our persecutors. Without telling the cop who answered the phone what group I represented, I asked if we needed a permit to march. He replied that a permit was required only if we intended to use sound equipment. We decided that wasn't necessary—we didn't expect a huge crowd, and we could yell loud enough without amps.

We showed up at the appointed time. I had been scared up to that point, thinking of MLK's assassination and of how many people hated us, but by the time I arrived at Washington Square Park the fear had evaporated. Marty Robinson and I led the participants around Greenwich Village, and then held a rally at Sheridan Square Park across the street from the Stonewall Inn. Later some participants said that this was the first time they had been openly gay, out in the sunshine.

According to a police report I read recently, the undercover cops assigned to keep an eye on us reported four hundred marchers. The reporter for the *Village Voice* estimated five hundred.

Once we had all gathered for the rally, Marty got up on the drinking fountain, above the crowd, and made a short speech. I jumped up next and said my piece. At the end, I looked out at the crowd and said, "We're not here to start another riot. Let's all go home peacefully. It's over for today, but this is just the beginning. We will be back!"

A year or so later, Marty Robinson and I had dinner together, during which he confessed to being a romantic who only wanted a good man to love him. I don't know if he ever found that love. He became cofounder of Gay Activists Alliance, was a founding member of ACT UP and other groups, and became famous for developing "zaps"—raucous public demonstrations— that targeted antigay politicians. He died of AIDS in 1992.

19

WE ARE THE GAY
LIBERATION FRONT!

AROUND THE TIME OF THAT FIRST GAY PROTEST MARCH, the more radical members of the traditional homophile organizations and some gay members of the leftist organizations began to meet at Alternate U. That institution, formerly known as the Free University of New York, occupied the second floor of a loft building on Fourteenth Street. I don't know how the people who ran it paid the rent, but tuition was twenty-four dollars for the first ten-week course and eight dollars for each additional course—or free, if you were on welfare. You could take classes or workshops in Marxism, self-defense, radical psychology, and so on; use the school's equipment to print fliers and broadsides; and hold meetings or dances in the big hall.

The spirit of the place—and of the times—was perhaps best characterized by the bathroom graffiti. High up on the wall someone had scrawled, "And God said e = mc². And there was a light show. Groovy!" Just above the roll of toilet paper, another person wrote, "Harvard diplomas. Take one."

I brought the name "Gay Liberation Front" to the second meeting of gays at Alternate U., and it was adopted unanimously. We were pretty freewheeling. There was no official membership—you just showed up—and there were no officers. People got together with others of like inclination and made things happen. We organized demonstrations, put on dances, and published a newspaper.

Bob Kohler was one of the people working to put on the dances. I remember him lugging in cracked ice and cases of beer, filling barrels with them, and selling the beer for twenty-five cents a can. That low price drew people away from the Mafia-run bars, which overcharged for watered-down drinks and made patrons pay extra for admission to a windowless inner room where you could slow dance with someone of your own sex. At our dances, nobody had to plunk coins in a jukebox—you could gyrate for free to rock music on the sound system, under the swirling light of a disco ball, until it was time to stagger home and let the cleanup crew sweep the floor.

We GLF women soon found that mixed dances didn't work for us. The gay men were involved with each other, oblivious of those few straight men who took advantage of the crowded floors to grope lesbians, so we arranged women-only dance nights. Now we could strip to the waist on hot summer nights, just as the men did. We danced in ecstatic circles, expressing a new sense of community, rather than coupling off.

Several Mafia thugs showed up at one of our first all-women's dances, guns in their belts, pretending to be cops. I guess their bosses were worried about losing business. They tried to intimidate the women and, according to Karla Jay, in her book *Tales of the Lavender Menace*, even punched some of them. I was cavorting in the middle of the dance floor and didn't even notice the confrontation. Meanwhile, someone had called Bob Kohler and also the local precinct. Bob arrived first, pretending to be Alternate U.'s manager, and got rid of the goons before the real cops showed up.

Later we moved our meetings to the basement of the Church of the Holy Apostles, an Episcopal parish on Ninth Avenue and Twenty-Eighth Street. Meetings could be raucous. Some people never said a word while others held forth at length. Lois Hart served as a moderator at times. At others Karla Jay was designated to keep order, which she did with a baseball bat in hand.

———————

My passion was the newspaper *Come Out!* I wrote opinion pieces and news stories, and typeset copy. Virginia let me use the cold-type machines after hours. She let other radical groups do the same, while she herself typeset the mailing list for the Black Panthers. The first edition of our paper appeared on November 14, 1969. We sold it for thirty-five cents.

Radical and counterculture newspapers proliferated throughout the United States during those years. Most were not profitable. I doubt we ever made money. After hawking copies on the street, I'd turn over the receipts to finance the next edition.

Our little publication made a big impression. Many articles were reprinted in other papers and anthologies, including one I wrote, "Stepin Fetchit Woman." The title wasn't my idea—whoever did the pasteup for that edition slapped it on. I thought it was sappy, but once it was in print I couldn't change it.

I hawked the paper on a corner in Greenwich Village, in my blue jeans and thrift-store suede jacket with a rip in the elbow, yelling, "Get your copy of *Come Out!*, newspaper of the Gay Liberation Front!" One day a well-dressed couple pushing a stroller passed by. They gave me that look-at-the-freak stare, so I added a few words to my pitch: "Find out what your kid's going to be like when he grows up!" They jumped. All right, it was unkind, but I couldn't help being pleased with myself.

Another chilly day, after selling papers for couple of hours, I ducked into a coffee shop and grabbed a seat at the counter, about three stools away from an NYU professor and one of his students. The professor was opining about feminism. In his estimation, more women entered paid employment nowadays because society needed a larger workforce. Feminist demands had nothing to do with it. We were merely froth on the tide of impersonal macroeconomic forces. I remember getting really angry with him. *Arrogant jerk*, I thought.

Today I admit he had a point. There has always been an interplay between the historic demands of the labor movement and women's movement on the one hand and the technological organization and power structure of society on the other. At the same time that women joined the labor market (while still shouldering most of the housework and childcare), the purchasing power of the average worker's wages inevitably declined until two incomes were needed where, previously, one income was enough to pay the rent and feed the children. Impersonal forces? No way. As Warren Buffett famously put it in 2006, "There's class warfare, all right, but it's my class, the rich class, that's making war, and we're winning."

On November 1, 1969, delegates from gay and lesbian groups met at the Eastern Regional Conference of Homophile Organizations (ERCHO) in Philadelphia. I attended as a representative of DOB, along with two other women. I was also, unofficially, there for GLF. At one point, the GLF delegation offered various proposals to the conference members, calling for support of such progressive/radical groups as the striking grape workers and the Panther 21. We also offered a platform based on the right to control one's own body. That included the right to have sex with other consenting adults, the right to *not* have your ass drafted and shipped to Vietnam, the right to ingest any drugs of your choice, and the rights to contraception and abortion.

The last item provoked a ferocious attack by Craig Schoonmaker of Homosexuals Intransigent, in which he denounced abortion as murder. I thought perhaps he was coming from a Catholic background, but later I found out that he simply hated women. The two other DOB women leaped to their feet, equally furious. I knew from private conversations that Allison had been raped and impregnated and had procured an illegal abortion. After this exchange, and certainly because of the DOB response, ERCHO voted overwhelmingly to accept the GLF platform.

In the long run, though, the most significant proposal came from Ellen Broidy of the NYU Student Homophile League and Craig Rodwell, owner of the Oscar Wilde Memorial Bookshop: to hold a march on the anniversary of the Stonewall Riots. That too was accepted, and the march took place on June 28, 1970. It subsequently morphed into the annual Gay Pride celebrations now held around the world, from Adelaide to Zurich—but not in Riyadh. At least not yet.

The most important thing I learned personally that day had to do with survival. I had been burning the candle at both ends, living on coffee, donuts, and meatball heroes, and not getting enough sleep. I ducked out of the conference to wash the grit off my face, glanced in the mirror—and then stared in horror at the blood oozing from my gums. *Cancer?* That smoking habit I had picked up from Louva—would it now cost me my life?

Immediately upon returning to NYC, I went to a clinic. The doctor took one look and asked, "Do you drink orange juice?"

He didn't have to say another word. I was mortified. All those biology classes in high school and college—and I had given myself scurvy.

The next day I filled the refrigerator with fresh fruit and vegetables. I went to the health food store and bought a hundred-pound sack of organic brown rice and hauled it up to my third-floor apartment. It would feed me through the winter.

In January 1970 there was an incident at Gianni's, a popular lesbian bar just north of the Village, when a couple of straight businessmen came in for drinks and saw two women dancing together. One of them tried to cut in but was rejected. He punched the butchier-looking woman, knocking her to the floor, and then left. The low-level Mafia guys, who owned the place and were supposed to provide security in exchange for their overpriced drinks, did nothing.

As soon as the news reached GLF, about fifteen of us, men and women, marched on the bar. We selected some fast tunes on the jukebox and danced in circles but did not order drinks. Once again, I was selected as spokesperson. Knees shaking, I went up to the owner and his partner. As I remember they were about a head and a half taller than I was and wore black pinstripe suits. Cinematic memories of Al Capone, machine guns, and the St. Valentine's Day massacre flickered in the back of my mind. Later I realized that they must have had frightening visions as well, of smashed furniture and liquor bottles, of thousands of dollars in uninsured damages.

After I'd finished chewing them out for not protecting the women who provided their livelihood, the taller one frowned down at me. "Do you know who *I* am?" he said.

"I don't know and I don't care," I shot back. "*We* are the Gay Liberation Front!" And I turned and walked back to the dance floor.

20

SOME PRIVATE AFFAIRS

WHILE I WAS BARRELING AHEAD into the newspaper and into radical politics, my love life crashed. The Stonewall Riots and formation of GLF had freed me from the notion that I should try to be bisexual. Meanwhile, however, Allison had taken a new lover—someone she had a great deal more in common with than she had with me.

Marion Youers—English by birth—was a textbook editor recently reassigned by her employer from Paris to New York. She showed up at DOB looking for congenial company. Allison was a technical writer. Marion was forty, Allison was forty-three. (I was a mere twenty-five—"a good kid," as Allison later described me to Marion.) In addition to their shared intellectual interests, they were both from strongly religious families. Allison was raised fundamentalist Christian, and Marion's grandfather was an Anglican minister. Each had discarded belief in a deity while retaining a strong moral sense—but these inclinations had taken them in opposite directions politically. Allison had become a Goldwater Republican, Marion a member of the Parti Communiste de France. By the time they got together, however, both of them had become disillusioned with those parties.

I was wounded when Allison and Marion formed an exclusive relationship. I was still somewhat under the influence of the Sullivanian nonmonogamy doctrine and hadn't realized how attached I had become to Allison. I said some hurtful things, and she stopped speaking to me for months.

Marion, however, didn't break off our friendship while Allison and I were on the outs, and in fact was very supportive of my political activities. We met during her lunch break in Midtown, keeping our meetings secret from Allison, and Marion recommended books. I dutifully slogged through Leonard Schapiro's magnum opus, *The Communist Party of the Soviet Union*, reading a few pages in bed every night until my eyes fell shut and the book fell out of my hands. The anarchist Bakunin was more to my liking.

I once asked Marion why she had joined the Communists. She said that at the time she believed Communism was the only way to ensure that, eventually, everyone would have enough to eat. This resonated with me. My mother had gone hungry in her youth, and once, when I had tried to talk politics with her, she had said, "I don't know anything about that. All I know is what every mother knows—that every child should have enough to eat."

Marion was still a Communist Party member when she arrived in the United States, and in fact belonged to a secret cell. It would have been dangerous for her to quit suddenly. What she did instead was to start asking questions when given an assignment. Eventually they stopped calling her and dropped her altogether.

Meanwhile, Jean Powers, head of the New York DOB, had become horrified by my leftward turn. She insisted that I meet with her, Marion, and Allison at the DOB office, where she interrogated me about my beliefs. Although Jean had been hounded out of government work when her superiors suspected her of being gay, she still wanted nothing more than acceptance into the mainstream, both as a lesbian and as a good, patriotic American. And now I, the person she'd picked to be public speaker for DOB, was turning into a Red.

I defended myself, saying I certainly wasn't joining any party or subordinating myself to its hierarchy. The others defended me as well. Occasionally Marion and I exchanged brief, amused glances. Jean would never have imagined that the very proper Englishwoman with the Maggie Smith R.P. accent was the real Communist in the room! Jean did, however, accept our explanations, and we remained friends.

I visited Jean occasionally during the next few years. I'm not sure how her relationship with Eleanor ended or why she stopped being involved with the Daughters of Bilitis. She started seeing a therapist who, instead of helping her through what must have been a difficult, lonely period, had a psychiatrist prescribe Thorazine. This medication has serious side effects and is normally used only for patients with severe mental illness, such as schizophrenia, the manic phase of bipolar disorder, or psychosis. Jean didn't have any of these conditions. Soon after starting the drug, she began to display the "Thorazine shuffle," a distinctive stiff-legged gait.

On one of those visits I met the therapist, who for some reason had come to Jean's apartment. Jean worshipped the woman. In my presence she literally knelt down and kissed her foot. I could see that the therapist reveled in her patient's adoration. It was also clear to me that she was exploiting Jean financially. I wanted to strangle her.

After I moved to the West Coast, I heard that Jean had died alone and wasn't discovered until a few days later. I never heard what caused her death. Allison, who had been her lover years before and was her last remaining friend, was called to identify the body. Marion told me it was a horrible, shattering experience.

I think what really killed Jean was the internalized self-hate so common to gays in those brutal times. Jean once told me a little about her early years. Her mother didn't show love for her and instead had tried to socialize her into being a Southern lady. The Defense Department, suspecting her of being gay, had driven her out, and she had stayed deep in the closet in subsequent employment. Because of her need to hide who she was, she couldn't get help for her mental health issues. She fought back with courage through all her work with DOB, but that wasn't enough to overcome a lifetime of antigay and misogynist cruelty. And the damage done by that predatory therapist slammed the lid on her coffin.

Watching Jean deteriorate increased the depth of my conviction that it was futile, even self-destructive, for gays to plead for acceptance from mainstream America. People say that it's better die on your feet than live on your knees. But even if you get down and crawl like a worm, they still won't let you live. They'll just step on you.

21

FIGHTING ON ALL FRONTS

THE GAY LIBERATION FRONT BROKE with its forebears in two ways. First, we didn't give a rat's ass about being respectable. We didn't want to move up in a system of hierarchical cruelties; we wanted to overturn it. Second, we made common cause with others fighting the same system.

Like many GLF members, I participated in a wide range of social justice actions.

In September 1969 I was part of the second feminist demonstration against the Miss America pageant. The first demonstration, held during the previous year, had disrupted the pageant, at least briefly, by unfurling a women's liberation banner. The second was a flop. Two women had purchased tickets to the show. I don't know what they planned to do if they succeeded in entering the convention center, but they had come up with the absurd plan to disguise themselves as nuns, using homemade costumes. Why would nuns want to attend a beauty contest? A large Irish security guard stopped them at the door and turned them away. He seemed amused.

We reconnoitered on the boardwalk. Robin Morgan, one of the organizers of the action, was desperate to salvage what she could. She called a press conference and announced, making it up as she went along, that we had called off our plan to disrupt the pageant because one of the contestants was secretly on our side. The pageant officials, she said, had discovered this and were holding the woman hostage and threatening her. With violence? Jail?—Robin didn't make that clear.

Once the reporters left, I took Robin aside. "But that was a lie!"

"History is a bunch of lies made up by men," she replied. "Let it be our lies for a change."

I was troubled by that. If we are known to be as dishonest as our oppressors, why should anyone trust us? Fortunately, none of the journalists picked up Robin's story.

Robin and I were pretty close in those days. At the time she was collecting material for an anthology, *Sisterhood Is Powerful*, and included my poem "Terror," and an essay, "Notes of a Radical Lesbian." When the book came out in 1970, I was dizzy with delight. Before that my work had only appeared in the DOB magazine, *The Ladder*, and in our GLF newspaper, *Come Out!* None of the contributors were paid, but that didn't matter. Over the decades since then, *Sisterhood Is Powerful* has been translated into I don't know how many languages, and I know my essay gave comfort to lesbians in other parts of the world.

In October 1969, according to the *New York Times*, over half a million people protested in Washington, DC, in the Moratorium to End the War in Vietnam. Smaller demonstrations took place all around the United States. In New York City, one arm of the protest marched across the Brooklyn Bridge to a rally on Wall Street. A GLF contingent was part of another gathering of forty thousand in Bryant Park, in the heart of midtown Manhattan. In my mind's eye I can still see our little band holding a banner aloft.

The next day liberal columnist Pete Hamill wrote about the event and described us as "the slim-waisted creeps of the Gay Liberation Front." Such bigotry was generally accepted at the time. Later, to his credit, Hamill apologized. "The kind of people who gravitate to tabloids—people like me, without great formal education—knew very little about the subject. . . . We had no idea."

In April of that year, twenty-one members of the Black Panther Party had been arrested, with bail set at $100,000 apiece. For the next ten months, the Panthers were held in solitary confinement. Lights were kept on twenty-four hours a day. The prisoners were denied reading materials, recreational facilities, and visits from family members. Some of them weren't even given mattresses. The two women were limited to four sheets of toilet paper per day. New Left groups, churches, and rich and famous individuals like Leonard Bernstein worked to raise the $2.1 million in bail money. In November, after much heated debate, GLF agreed to donate $500 to the fund. I was on the losing side—I thought we were such a small organization, with so little in our piggy bank, that we should keep it for our own needs. Also, at that time the Panthers were distinctly homophobic, slamming their enemies as "faggots." In retrospect, I was wrong. The next year, when GLF members confronted the Panthers at their convention, they changed their policies regarding gays.

On December 4, 1969, the Chicago police murdered two Panthers, Fred Hampton and Mark Clark, shooting over ninety times into the apartment where the men slept. When I heard the news, I was terrified. *They could do that to any of us*, I thought. Afraid to stay alone, I spent the next night at the apartment of GLFers Lois Hart and Suzanne Bevier. Their presence comforted me.

On December 7, thirteen representatives of the Young Lords, a Puerto Rican liberation group, went to the First Spanish Methodist Church in East Harlem to request space for a children's breakfast program. The minister called the police, who beat the thirteen and arrested them on charges of "inciting to riot." On December 28, the Young Lords entered the church and occupied it for the next ten days. They used the premises for the breakfast program, classes, film showings, a free clinic staffed by a sympathetic doctor and medical students, and a New Year's Mass by a radical priest.

As a representative of GLF I visited the church and the Young Lords office a couple of times. They were aware of the Stonewall Riots and were already in support. Jon, another GLFer, was working with the Young Lords, as were two women's liberation activists and a representative of the United Farm Workers. My article reporting on the Young Lords action appeared in the next issue of *Come Out!*

During Christmas week, GLF held a vigil outside the Women's House of Detention for the two women imprisoned as part of the

Panther group, Joan Bird and Angela Davis. I had a late-night shift, and it was very cold. Just as I was about to leave, a couple who lived in the area invited some of us to their townhouse to warm up. They were obviously wealthy liberals, with leftist posters on their walls. They fed us things we could never afford to buy. That wheel of brie on the table must have been a foot and a half in diameter.

The trial of the Panther 21 took eight months. In May 1971, after what had been the longest and costliest trial in New York history, the defendants were acquitted of all charges. Taxpayers footed the bill, and the cops and the FBI continued to target the Panthers.

We lost a member in 1970, when Lydia French was murdered. We were told that she let someone into her apartment, and he shot her in the back of the head. We knew that her father was a right-wing army officer, and that he was appalled to find what his daughter had become— not only a lesbian but also a member of that "commie" group, the GLF. At around the same time as the murder, he left the country and was reported to be in Canada. As far as I know, he never returned, and the United States never requested his extradition.

The New York City police came to a GLF meeting, asking for bits of information that might help them find the perpetrator. No one came forward. None of us had a clue, but even if we had, why would we give it to people who might turn around and use it against us? The sworn officers were our sworn enemies.

In April 1970, three years before *Roe v. Wade*, abortion became legal in New York State. During those three years, women from other parts of the country and from Canada traveled to New York to terminate their pregnancies. I worked with an organization helping them, putting one of the women up in my apartment after a saline injection until she expelled the fetus. My friend Barbara Joans tells me she let thirty such visitors stay on her couch, "though not all at the same time."

By 1970 I'd known quite a number of women who'd had illegal abortions in previous years. As I wrote in an earlier chapter, the first was my mother's. The second was in 1961, a thirteen-year-old girl who'd been raped by her grandfather. The nurse who attended her was in my judo class at the YWCA and told me about it during a ride home on the subway. She said that the doctors at her hospital scheduled D&Cs "to remove fibroids" one day a week, providing compassionate care to women like my mother and that raped child. When I was in Sullivanian therapy, trying to be bisexual, we all knew that we could get help with an unwanted pregnancy by seeing "Dr. Spencer in Pennsylvania."

Over the years, numerous friends and lovers, both straight and lesbian, told me they'd had abortions. Three of them, including Allison, had been raped. Two had been seduced and abandoned by their college professors. A few had undergone the procedure as teenagers, because they and the fathers were too young to support children. And others simply mentioned that they too had aborted, without sharing the circumstances.

After the *Roe v. Wade* decision, during a trip to Chicago, I interviewed a member of the Jane Collective, the underground abortion service. These women, none of them medical personnel, had learned to perform D&Cs themselves, helping thousands of others—and only one of the thousands developed an infection and needed hospitalization.

22

RAT NEWSPAPER—AND SOME REAL RATS

RAT AND *COME OUT!*, our Gay Liberation Front newspaper, were two of more than a thousand "underground" papers published in the United States during the Vietnam War era.

In January 1970 a collective of women had approached *RAT Subterranean News*, a.k.a. *RAT*, an underground newspaper that was politically left but extremely sexist, as were so many similar papers of that time. The women had presented the guys with the idea of producing a feminist issue, presumably to show how it could be done, and in February I was invited to join them as the radical lesbian in the group. Of course I said yes!

Our collective did publish a feminist issue of *RAT*, but then, instead of handing the paper back to the men, we kept it. We changed the paper's name to *Women's LibeRATion*. We were a rather motley crowd. Some, like writer Robin Morgan and graphic artist Susan Simensky, had already been involved with feminist organizations. Others came directly from the radical left. Carol Grosberg had been to Cuba and was a big fan of their revolution. Jane Alpert was out on bail, charged with bombing eight government and corporate buildings. Sharon Krebs was one of the founders of the experimental Free University of New York, where professors who'd been dismissed for socialist or antiwar views could teach.

I never learned about Miriam Rosen's previous involvements, but after *RAT* she went on to produce programming at Pacifica Radio. Wendy R., who I think was the youngest, didn't quite fit in. She was something of a yippie and wanted to make a revolution for joy.

I don't remember all the others. I studiously avoided the two who called themselves Suzie Weatherwoman and Judy Weatherwoman, thinking that if I were arrested and subjected to torture—excuse me, "enhanced interrogation"—I didn't want to have any information the cops could squeeze out of me. For those who don't remember, the Weather Underground Organization believed we needed a violent revolution to end America's imperialist wars and its capitalist exploitation and racism at home. They set off a total of twenty-five bombs, mostly small, during their existence, generally in the bathrooms of government offices and corporation headquarters.

Our smoke-filled meetings were very intense, our conversations larded with references to Third World revolutions, both past and in progress, and the need for sacrifice. On one occasion Jane Alpert declared that the Vietnamese guerillas subsisted on a bowl of rice a day yet were still winning the war. In that charged atmosphere I set aside everything I'd learned about nutrition—including my own experience with vitamin deficiency—and believed her, at least for the moment.

We published articles championing those revolutions, including a rose-colored one by Robin Morgan about women in Mao's China. The Weatherwomen contributed a piece calling for armed struggle against the US government. We reported on the Vietnam War, the trial of the Panther 21, and the role of women activists in the peace movement and various international conflicts. I haven't been able to find archived copies of the paper or any of its articles, except for Morgan's piece, "Goodbye to All That," which denounced the sexism of the male left and has since become a classic, and Marge Piercy's poem, "Metamorphosis into Bureaucrat." I also found the seven-panel cartoon I drew for the first women's issue—and "Gay Is Good," an article I wrote that has been translated into other languages and anthologized worldwide. I didn't choose this title either, and consider it even more sappy than the titles foisted on any of my other articles.

Wendy needed a place to stay and moved into my Lower East Side slum apartment. When we were alone, she summarized all the neo-Marxist dogma by squatting as if constipated. "Struggle, struggle," she grunted. I had to laugh. But her lack of a hard-left ideology brought her under suspicion. One day Alpert called a meeting of the collective. Convinced that Wendy was an FBI agent, she led a purge and drove the youngster from the paper. I protested, to no avail. Alpert criticized me for being a humanist, describing herself proudly as a Stalinist.

In May 1970, a month before being sentenced, Alpert jumped bail and went underground. She and her boyfriend Sam Melville had been betrayed by an agent, George Demmerle.

In December 1970 Sharon Krebs was arrested for attempting to bomb a bank, along with her boyfriend Robin Palmer and some members of Weatherman. They'd been betrayed by an agent named Steve.

Those were violent times, abroad and at home. President Nixon, elected on his promise that he had a "secret plan" to end the Vietnam War, escalated it instead, mercilessly bombing both Cambodia and Laos. My government was committing genocide. Sometimes I wondered why I wasn't building bombs. Shouldn't I be willing to risk my life and freedom to stop it? Was I just a coward?

One day as I was coming home, the elderly Ukrainian lady who lived on the second floor stopped me in the hallway. We had spoken on previous occasions about the deaths of her abusive husband and of her beloved cat. (She mourned the cat but not the husband.) This time she had a warning for me. "The FBI was here asking questions about you. I didn't tell them nothing." Not that she had anything to tell them—I'd never discussed politics with her. But I understood why a refugee from the Soviet police state would be loath to inform on a neighbor.

Another day a young man asked me up to his apartment to plan an action. He showed me a .22 caliber rifle and then talked about killing people by inserting poison in their cigarettes. The alarm in my brain screamed *Agent! Agent!* I left as fast as I could.

I don't remember how many months I worked on the paper, but I know I wasn't part of the collective that published the July 14–23, 1971, issue. It included an article accusing Virginia Ruffalo of being a government agent. I never met Ruffalo. Some months later, while visiting a friend in Boston, I did meet with a few local feminists. They told me that they had taken Ruffalo to a safe house in another state and interrogated her for a few days before letting her go.

"Are you crazy?" I said. "Kidnapping someone across state lines is a capital offense. If she really was an agent, you'd all be behind bars and headed for death row." I was thinking of the Federal Kidnapping Act (Lindbergh Law) of 1932. Although I wasn't aware of it at the time, the Supreme Court in 1968 had removed the death penalty from that law, as long as the victim hadn't been physically harmed.

The paper folded in 1972, perhaps for lack of funds, perhaps because so many of us had gone in different directions—underground, to other groups, or to prison. Looking back on those paranoid days, I can't help but notice a pattern. Jane Alpert and Sharon Krebs were working with their boyfriends when they bombed or attempted to bomb corporate and government buildings. They were betrayed by male agents—guys they hadn't suspected. Their suspicion, and that of their comrades on *RAT*, fell instead on other women.

23

OCCUPYING THE PORN FACTORY

NINETEEN SEVENTY WAS A BUSY YEAR. Besides working on *Come Out!*, the Gay Liberation Front newspaper, and on *RAT* newspaper after we women took it over, I participated in three building occupations and the Lavender Menace action at the National Organization for Women conference.

The first building occupation was on April 13, 1970, when nine women barricaded ourselves in the executive offices of Grove Press. Barney Rosset, who owned the press, had gained an avant-garde reputation by publishing books that were censored for sexual content, including *Lady Chatterley's Lover* and the writings of the Marquis de Sade, as well as radical treatises such as Frantz Fanon's *The Wretched of the Earth*, *The Autobiography of Malcolm X*, and New Left political literature.

However, this radical bent did not extend to supporting workers' rights. When eight employees signed union cards, Rosset fired them. At the same time that we feminists took over the offices, the union was holding a street protest outside. Our occupation was in response both to the firings and to the company's sexism. As our lawyer Emily Goodman put it, "Grove Press won't let women be anything but secretaries, scrubwomen, and sex symbols."

Robin Morgan, who led us, was one of those fired by Rosset. The rest of us were members of various women's liberation groups, and Morgan had called on us for support. The only other name I remember is that of Ti-Grace Atkinson, who had founded a group called the Feminists.

Once inside, we used a heavy desk to block the office door, hung a banner out the window, and called the press. Then we waited. I looked around at the fancy furniture, Rosset's private shower room, and his liquor cabinet. Although I'm not a drinker, in the revolutionary spirit of Fanon I helped myself to a shot of Rosset's whiskey.

Rosset called the police, of course. They shoved their way in and arrested us. Morgan refused to move and made them carry her downstairs. I didn't want them to touch me, so I walked. They drove us around town, from one station to another, not letting our attorney know where we were, and finally fingerprinted and booked us.

We were put in a holding pen along with three or four prostitutes. We were White, and they were Black. One of them was coming down from heroin. She lay on the bench in a fetal position, shivering uncontrollably. She was going cold turkey, because if she admitted to using heroin and asked for help with the symptoms, they would put her in a treatment center for thirty days. When she got out, her pimp would probably beat her. If all she had to face was a charge of prostitution, the judge would fine her, and she'd be back working the streets in the morning. Ti-Grace was obviously horrified by the woman's situation. She held her in her lap, covered her with a jacket, and caressed her head.

Another prostitute, Peaches, was cheerful and philosophical. She saw all sex—at least with men—as transactional. "Jackie O. sells it, too," she declared. Just to one rich man at a time.

Night had fallen and none of us had eaten. One of our group said she had stress diabetes, and if she didn't get food pretty soon she would pass out. Just about then a cop came in and announced that we'd all have to be strip-searched. After a quick caucus, we told him that we would submit peacefully only if they brought our friend something to eat. They sent a nice young officer to the grocery, and he returned with a candy bar, which sufficed.

They separated us for the search. It was hateful, humiliating—the police matron stared at me like I was dirt. Ti-Grace, however, wouldn't cooperate. The cops handcuffed her to cell bars and stripped her forcibly.

As it happened, most of us were on our periods at the time, and as a further indignity the matrons took away our tampons. Then we were put into individual cells, to sleep if we could on hard wooden benches, without any bedding, oozing blood into our underpants. In the morning we were given bologna sandwiches on stale white bread and a choice of either cold milk or dishwater coffee. I don't remember which I chose.

We were taken to the judge, who let us go on our own recognizance. My friend Marion Youers, who had been jailed in Paris for sheltering Algerian women during the French-Algerian war, was there at the courthouse. She had taken off from work and brought all the cash she had on hand, intending to bail me out. Fortunately, that wasn't necessary.

A few days after the occupation, a tall, stunningly gorgeous woman showed up at the *RAT* office. She told us that she had been working as a call girl, and on one occasion Rosset engaged her services. However, sadistic abuse was not part of the deal, and that was what he inflicted on her. Given Grove's history of publishing sadomasochistic literature, and Rosset's statement that he chose books because they turned him on, I wasn't surprised.

In subsequent arbitration, Rosset rehired most of the fired union workers, but when a vote to actually establish a union failed, he fired half the staff again. He never did meet any of the feminist demands, which included childcare for employees, profits from *The Autobiography of Malcolm X* to go to the Black community, and profits from his misogynist publications to go to programs that helped victimized women. But the occupation changed the public discourse, at least in more liberal circles, from defending porn as free speech to questioning how it reinforced male domination and what we now call rape culture.

I was in a bloody rage for weeks. I knew very well that because the nine of us who were arrested were White, with media connections, we had not been treated all that badly. Still, I also knew that I never wanted to be in the cops' power again, never again to be put in a cage and have them decide when and what I ate and whether I could have menstrual supplies. Ever since then I have been unable to understand the conscientious objectors who, during the Vietnam War, chose a prison term instead of fleeing to Canada.

Shortly after the Grove Press episode, I made a fiery speech denouncing the police and the government they serve. A young man from Phoenix heard that speech, and in 1972 he invited me to speak at the University of Arizona in Tempe. But that would be two years later, and there were other battles closer on the horizon.

24

A MENACE GRABS
THE MIC

I DON'T KNOW WHO CAME UP with the idea of confronting the National Organization for Women (NOW) about its homophobia. Betty Friedan, a founder of NOW, deserves some credit for referring to lesbians as the "Lavender Menace."

Friedan also deserves credit for waking my confused nineteen-year-old self (and myriads of other women) to feminism with her book *The Feminine Mystique*; for co-founding NOW, the National Women's Political Caucus, and the National Abortion Rights Action League (NARAL); and for a lifetime of work on behalf of our sex. I was a dues-paying member of NOW for a couple of years and met quite a few friends at their conferences.

Friedan and many of her associates wanted nothing more than the opportunity to join the mainstream, as the NOW mission statement put it, "in truly equal partnership with men." Their desire for mainstream acceptance was one it shared with the early homophile organizations. Both rejected socialist and antiwar politics for fear of being tarred as "commies." But nothing could panic the leadership of NOW more than the idea of being dismissed as a bunch of man-hating dykes.

On May 1, 1970, NOW's Second Congress to Unite Women opened in the auditorium of a junior high school in Manhattan. A couple hundred women filed in and took their seats—forty GLF members scattered anonymously among them.

The panelists on stage had been selected to discuss the problems facing women in different positions in society—one was a union member, another represented a Black women's association, and so on. Just as the moderator was about to open the conference, the lights went out. GLF members Jessie Falstein and Michela Griffo, who had cased the joint the day before, had flipped the switches. They waited a few moments and then turned the lights back on.

Under cover of darkness, we had taken off our outer shirts to display hand-stenciled T-shirts that read LAVENDER MENACE. We had taped signs on the auditorium walls with slogans like TAKE A LESBIAN TO LUNCH and LAVENDER JANE LOVES YOU. We then handed out copies of a manifesto that a group of us had written collectively, *The Woman-Identified Woman*. In the decades since then it has become a classic, reprinted and distributed worldwide.

My job was to jump up on the stage and grab the mic. I explained that we were here because lesbians had been excluded, and we wanted to talk about our issues. Then I put it to the audience. "Let's take a vote—how many want to continue with the panel discussion? How many want to hear what we have to say?" The women voted overwhelmingly to hear from us. Then other Menaces marched down the aisle and stepped up onto the stage, while a few remained in the audience. A freewheeling discussion ensued.

At their next annual conference NOW revised their platform to include lesbian rights.

Although I didn't know it at the time, the use of that junior high school had been arranged by NOW member Barbara Joans, whose sons were students there. She did that for NOW's first conference there as well—she met with the principal and wangled the place for free. At that first conference, male reporters tried to bulldoze their way in, but the women fought back and managed to keep them and their cameras out. Barbara and Rita Mae Brown snatched the tape from one of the newsreel guys who had barged in, and then they ran out of the building and threw it down the nearest sewer.

I grab the mic at the Lavender Menace action. *Photo by Diana Davies, Manuscripts and Archives Division, The New York Public Library*

In 1970 Barbara joined the Christopher Street Gay Liberation Day March. As a graduate student in anthropology, she confronted the psychological establishment at a different conference, insisting that homosexuality was an identity and not a disorder. I met her in 1971, and we've been close friends ever since. Dr. Joans, by the way, is incurably heterosexual.

The second time I grabbed the mic was at the Women's Strike event on August 26, 1970. Friedan herself had organized this event—a march culminating in a rally at Bryant Park. Bryant Park is the public space behind the New York Public Library's main branch and has been called Manhattan's town square. I understand the event was originally supposed to be an actual strike, but in fact the participants weren't expected to abandon their jobs. Since it was a weekday, the march was set to start at 5:30 PM so they could join in after work.

Although the city refused to block off vehicular traffic for the march, ten to twenty thousand women showed up, filling all lanes on Fifth Avenue. The police were unable to restrict us to one side. According to the *New York Times*, the speakers at the rally included Friedan, Eleanor Holmes Norton, Bella Abzug, Gloria Steinem, the male deputy mayor, Kate Millett, and a Black woman who was representing the Third World Women's Alliance, but whom the *Times* didn't name. I was behind the stage and not listening to the speeches—I already knew I'd agree with them—so I didn't get her name either.

There was one unofficial speaker.

No lesbian had been invited to address the rally. Kate Millett was in fact a lesbian, but she wasn't out to the media at that time. I approached the circle of women protecting the stage—they had linked arms—and asked to talk to Millett. They refused to let me through. I put up my fists. "If you don't," I said, "there's going to be a fight, right in front of the press. You want that on TV tonight?"

One of the women called Millett, who escorted me up onto the platform and let me have the mic after she had delivered her remarks. I didn't give my name, just announced that we'd seen some recent assaults on lesbians in the streets of NYC, and I'd come on their behalf and on behalf of all the other anonymous lesbians who suffered discrimination and persecution in this country.

I made at least one good impression. Some months later I met June Walker, who told me she had been electrified by my speech. An upper-middle-class woman in an unhappy marriage, she had put on a nice summer dress and gone to the rally with a lesbian friend who had a crush on her. Nothing came of that crush, but Walker and I had a fling, until she moved to Los Angeles.

Sometime in 1970 I was invited to represent GLF on a TV program in Toronto. I had asked if they would put me up with a local women's group, thinking it would be a way to meet other feminists and would save the station money, but they put me in a hotel instead.

The program was called *Firing Line* (no relation to William Buckley's conservative talk show here in the United States). When I arrived at the studio, the host's female assistant escorted me to what felt like a bear pit. I was in the center, on ground level, with a ring of elevated podia around me. A cop stood behind the first podium, a clergyman behind a second, a Mrs. Somebody-or-Other at the third, and waffle-y kind of guy at the fourth. For the first part of the show, they fired angry remarks at me, the queer. Before one stopped speaking, the next would open fire, without giving me a chance to utter a syllable in reply.

Mrs. Somebody-or-Other was the worst. She apparently had several children and was unhappy with her life and furious with me. She accused me of just wanting to enjoy sex, party, and be irresponsible.

Intermission came, with a chance to catch my breath. I told the host that I had something to say, and when he opened the second half, he let me address my tormentors. "I've never been to Canada before. I'm your guest here. This can't be an example of Canadian hospitality. How about letting me speak?" From then on the show was mine.

After the taping, I went back to the hotel room, called a local feminist organization, and invited whoever was in the office up for dinner, putting it on *Firing Line*'s account.

25

NO GAY DANCING
ALLOWED

On September 20, 1970, a pleasant Sunday evening, we were holding our regular Gay Liberation Front meeting at the Church of the Holy Apostles when Ellen Broidy burst into the room and asked for help.

Ellen was president of the Student Homophile League (SHL) at New York University. She had run the two miles from NYU to the church. She told us that her group had contracted with the student council in charge of Weinstein Hall, the freshman dorm, to put on a gay dance in the subbasement. The administration had gotten wind of the agreement and vetoed it.

NYU students had gone on strike a year before and, among other things, won the right to run their own dormitories. The freshmen ran theirs, the sophomores theirs, and so on. Now it seemed that their rights were contingent on the administration's approval. The dorm council and the SHL were conferring at that very hour, and the SHL was asking for our support.

Several of us followed Ellen back to the university. Once we joined the meeting, she explained to us that the president of the college had made an offer. He would hire a psychiatrist to declare that gay people were mentally disturbed. The SHL would hire a psychiatrist to present the opposite view. The president would listen to both sides and then decide about the dance.

Did he think the students would be stupid enough to take him up on his offer, or that they would just slink away after such an obvious slap in the face? The dance was scheduled for Friday. After some discussion, and with GLF support, the dorm council and the SHL voted to hold it anyway.

Worried about how this was likely to play out, I spoke up. "Let's say we advertise the dance for Friday night. That evening there'll be cops at the door, and we'll never get in. We have to occupy the subbasement now and hold it for the rest of the week."

All present agreed. Some of us from GLF ran back to the church to collect the rest of our members. One GLFer hightailed it over to Alternate U. with instructions to write up a flier and print copies on their mimeograph machine. The flier would be passed around campus, explaining our actions. Arthur Bell, who wrote for the *Village Voice*, waited outside the building. The minute we returned, he would call the press.

As the GLF group marched back to NYU, some street queens joined us. Soon we were all camped out in the subbasement of Weinstein Hall. We made ourselves as comfortable as possible. There were chairs, tables, vending machines, and a laundry room. For the young gays who'd been thrown out by their families and were struggling to survive on the streets, I imagine it was a relief to have a roof over their heads and not have to turn a trick that night. I was young enough then to not mind sleeping on the floor, and happy to share a blanket with one of the queens. Soon enough we were all huddling under whatever covers we could scrounge, because the administration turned up the air-conditioning in an attempt to freeze us out. For six days we came and went for meals or work or to attend classes.

During this time, some of the freshmen upstairs were not happy about the invasion. We held another meeting, this one open to all the residents of the dorm. I remember explaining that we weren't just fighting for ourselves but also to defend the right of self-governance that the students had won the previous year. This satisfied them.

Me selling copies of *Come Out!* during our occupation of Weinstein Hall. *Photo by Diana Davies, Manuscripts and Archives Division, The New York Public Library*

On Friday I thought I might be catching a cold, so I went home for a hot bath—and missed the denouement. The administration called the police, who arrested everyone in the subbasement. One of the street queens had been doing laundry and was naked except for a blanket, but the cops wouldn't let her collect her clothes. They loaded her bare-assed into the paddy wagon.

Despite the hot bath, I caught the cold—and a case of crabs from sharing that blanket.

Sylvia Rivera was one of those arrested. I hadn't seen her at GLF before, but she attended a meeting after the occupation, and I had a conversation with her. The events had inspired her to form a new organization—Street

Transvestite Action Revolutionaries (STAR). STAR cofounder Marsha P. Johnson, I learned later, also participated in the Weinstein Hall action, not inside the hall but picketing outside.

Later, I heard from another GLFer that some gay freshmen at Weinstein Hall were inspired by the event to come out.

Although we failed to hold the subbasement that Friday night, the uproar we caused forced the administration to make its peace with a changing society, and a gay dance was held the following year. Now NYU has an LGBTQ+ center, and in 2020 they marked the fiftieth anniversary of the occupation by putting on a panel discussion.

26

"YOU'RE ON THE WRONG SIDE!"

I DIDN'T GET BUSTED AT WEINSTEIN HALL, despite having instigated the occupation. However, I got another chance to get arrested on New Year's Eve, when a handful of women took over an abandoned welfare center on the Lower East Side, right across from the Fifth Street police station.

Nineteen seventy was drawing to a close when a member of a radical feminist group phoned to invite me to an action. We would meet at their office on New Year's Eve. She told me to wear warm clothes and bring a sleeping bag if I had one. She wouldn't say what they were planning or where we'd be going.

A dozen women were there when I arrived. After a short pep talk, and without giving us any more information, the organizers led us out into the night.

A light snow drifted down on us as we marched eastward, single file, from the office in lower Manhattan. Other people might be having boisterous parties indoors or gathering in Times Square to watch the ball drop, but East Fifth Street was very, very quiet.

Our guides took us to a building that had been a welfare center until the city stopped using it and let it fall into disrepair. It was massive, covering the whole block or at least most of it. The ground-floor windows were broken. The organizers had picked the lock before we arrived. They had also hauled in a few propane heaters, but these were next to useless in that cavernous hall. Still, if you stayed close enough— but not so close that your bedroll caught fire—the heaters were better than nothing. The concrete floor felt like a frozen lake under my sleeping bag, and the wind moaned through the broken panes.

The plan, we were told, was to reclaim the property and turn it into a women's center, with a focus on serving the poor—which was just about everyone who lived on the Lower East Side back then. The next day somebody brought in clothes racks from a store that had gone out of business, and soon we had hung them with donated sweaters and other clothes. Word spread quickly. Within hours neighbors arrived to pick over the freebies. Other women came by to help, including a statuesque redhead who put herself to work sweeping up trash. Someone whispered to me that she was Marion Tanner, the wealthy aunt of author Patrick Dennis, and the model for the Auntie Mame immortalized in his novel by that name. Was it really her? I never found out.

My place was just a few blocks north, so I decided to go home for a hot bath. Mikki, a young woman I'd been chatting with, asked if she could join me since she lived in Queens, a long subway ride away. I said sure. (Mikki's birth name was Mary McCarthy, and she later went back to using that.)

My current tenement apartment had a bathtub in the kitchen, with a cover of enameled tin. The cover served as a counter for meal preparation, and I took it off to bathe. The toilet was a closet so small my knees bumped against the door when I shut it, and I'm pretty short. The bedroom was just about big enough to hold the loft bed I had cobbled together. Since I'm no carpenter, it creaked and swayed whenever I turned over. But with this addition I had room to shove a desk and chair underneath.

Somehow, after the bath, Mikki and I ended up in bed together. Later I learned that she'd had her eye on me for a while, but I was too oblivious to notice. She *was* young, though of age at eighteen and no longer what we then called "jailbait" (I was twenty-six). She had short blonde hair, freckles, a quick mind, and a fiery spirit. We were lovers for about nine months and, despite occasional spats, remain friends even now, bonded for life.

We returned to the old welfare center in the morning, having lots of work to do. We intended to provide the community with free meals and a health clinic. Our plans hit a roadblock, however, when the police came in and arrested us. This time they didn't run us around the city in paddy wagons, or fingerprint, strip-search, and humiliate us. The building our leaders had picked for us to occupy just happened to be right across the street from the precinct house, so the cops simply escorted us over. And since the city had more or less abandoned the building, they didn't need to "teach us a lesson," the way they had when we barricaded ourselves into the executive offices of Grove Press. After all, we weren't trespassing on any rich man's property.

We spent the afternoon with the arresting officers. One of them kept trying to get us to admit that we'd broken the law, but we avoided any confession of wrongdoing. Finally, I asked, "Why are you bothering the women's movement? You should be going after the Mafia instead of us."

He gave me a disgusted look. "Listen, sister," he said in a New York accent so pure you could use it as a down payment on the Brooklyn Bridge, "the government is the Mafia, and the Mafia is the government. And the trouble with you"—he stabbed the air in my direction—"is you're on the wrong side!"

An honest cop. I was impressed. They released us without charges.

———————————

We didn't get to keep that old welfare center, which probably would have cost over a million dollars to repair. But the organizers negotiated with the city and were able to purchase an unused firehouse, in somewhat better shape, for one dollar. It had a spiral staircase. We called it the Women's Liberation Center, and we had it from 1972 to 1987. In 2019 it was designated a historic landmark.

Soon after a group of feminists purchased the firehouse, I was asked to attend a meeting. It seemed that women from the Socialist Workers Party (SWP) were attempting to have members of their cadre run for president, treasurer, and so on of the group that ran the building. By then the SWP had a history of infiltrating and taking over other organizations and diverting funds to the party's purposes. As I recollect, somewhere between fifty and a hundred of us showed up to stop them. During the discussion I proposed a resolution that no official of any registered political party could hold those positions. One of the SWP women objected, saying that we were discriminating against them. I pointed out that the resolution would apply equally to Democratic and Republican officials—and that the SWP's own regulations barred gays from their organization.

My resolution passed overwhelmingly. The following summer I was visiting Marge Piercy on Cape Cod, when the SWP tried to take over their local women's liberation group. I attended a meeting there as well, told the story of the firehouse, and helped defeat them.

Later that year, at their national convention, they changed their antigay policy.

27

THE RADICAL RADISHES

As part of the Lavender Menace action, we had called for consciousness-raising (C-R) groups. Women from the NOW conference—some of whom were already lesbians, others starting to explore their feelings—joined those of us already in GLF to form four C-R groups. I was in the second group. When we met, we'd pick a topic, anything to do with growing up female in a patriarchal society. Then we'd go around the room and each share her story. The idea was that we would learn to listen to and respect another woman's experiences.

On the negative side, though, being in C-R group #1 (with published authors like Kate Millett) conferred a higher status than being in #2, being in #2 was higher status than #3, and #3, of course, beat #4. Despite our ideology, within the women's movement we could not manage to escape the hierarchical structure of the surrounding society.

Since we had joined forces with the NOW women and were meeting separately from GLF, we could no longer call ourselves "GLF women," so early in 1971 we began using the name Radicalesbians. Our new organization tried to remain leaderless. We maintained the tradition of going around the room to ensure that everyone—not just the loud-mouths like me—had a chance to speak. Another policy was that we needed complete consensus before undertaking any action. This meant that one woman's *no* vote would paralyze the group.

And it did. Time after time, we'd come up with an idea and take a vote. And each time, Pat Maxwell would veto the proposal. She never gave a reason, never put forth any proposals of her own. She was obviously enjoying herself. One day she showed her contempt by presenting us with buttons she'd designed: a drawing of two radishes, their tails entwined, and the words RADICAL RADISHES.

During this period Rita Mae Brown and I were close. What we wanted was a revolutionary feminist organization, so we wrote a paper outlining its structure and policies. I don't think we ever presented this document at a Radicalesbians meeting. Our fantasies were perhaps a bit out of touch with reality—such a manifesto would have been met with polite blank looks before the women turned to another topic.

28

MY BRIEF RADIO CAREER

EARLY IN 1972 NANETTE RAINONE, program director at WBAI-FM, asked me if I'd be interested in doing a lesbian show. Would I ever! I knew nothing about radio production but jumped at the chance. She told me to come in for training.

WBAI—for those who've never lived in NYC—is a member of the Pacifica Network of noncommercial, listener-supported stations. Given the lack of advertising revenue, most of us who worked there were volunteers. Rainone had created some of its first feminist programs and was the first woman to become program director there.

She assigned me to work with Gary Fried, another volunteer and one of the few gay people at the station. He told me to buy a cassette recorder, then showed me how to transfer cassette to reel-to-reel, how to edit tape on those reels using the editing block, a razor blade, and adhesive splicing tape, and how to fade in music. Such was the technology of the time.

My half-hour program, *Lesbian Nation*, came on the air every Friday evening from 1972 to 1974. (Jill Johnston's book with the same title was published in 1973.) What with arranging to meet guests, taping them, and then editing the results, I spent twenty hours per week producing the show. It became my new (unpaid) part-time job.

I interviewed feminist authors, most of whom were obliging enough to read from their work. These included Esther Newton, Bertha Harris, Audre Lorde, Marge Piercy, Myrna Lamb, Frances Doughty, Phyllis Chesler, Jill Johnston, Barbara Love, and Sydney Abbott. When Judy Grahn came to town, I recorded her at the Women's Liberation Center. Her magnificent elegy *A Woman Is Talking to Death* knocked my socks off, and I ended the show by segueing into Babatunde Olatunji's *Drums of Passion*. Apparently listeners were blown away as well, because they responded with a flurry of contributions to the station.

When I left New York, I donated tapes of my shows to the Lesbian Herstory Archives. Reel-to-reel tapes degrade over time, so the archive has been digitizing them.

During those *Lesbian Nation* years, I carried my mic to demonstrations. One of these was by men protesting laws requiring the payment of alimony (now known as spousal support). The National Organization for Women staged a counterprotest in favor of alimony laws and increasing child support. I interviewed both groups.

A different kind of demonstration, of martial arts and self-defense, took place at the new women's center. The instructor explained what she was doing as she showed the moves, and I scrambled around her, pointing the mic at the mat as she threw a would-be attacker: *Thud! Pow! Ki-ai!* Her running description and sound effects were sufficient; you didn't need visuals to get a kick out of the show.

Another show was a sportscast from a feminist softball game, with interviews of the participants.

When Sharon Krebs was released from a three-year sentence after a failed attempt at bombing to protest the war, I invited her to the studio. A brilliant woman, she had lots to say about the way our prison system treats female inmates. She later taught a course on the subject at the New School for Social Research.

In June 1973, when Jane Alpert, wanted for radical bombings in New York, sent out her manifesto *Mother Right* from underground, I read it on the air. That September I read the response to Alpert from women of the Weather Underground. *Ms.* magazine published Alpert's manifesto in 1974.

Working at WBAI changed my life in many ways. Nanette Rainone and Gary Fried are deceased, and I regret never thanking them enough for giving me that opportunity.

Shortly after I started my program at WBAI, I began looking for another place to live. I kept getting robbed, even after having the building super-intendent put iron gates on the windows and a police lock on the door. The super, it turned out, was an addict—his wife admitted it to me—and that was why I was being robbed. Only after she told me that did I notice the track marks on the backs of his hands. Another former member of the *RAT* collective, Miriam Rosen, had also joined the radio station, and at the time that I needed new digs, she happened to be giving up what she called her "squalorific slum apartment." I took it.

Rita Mae and I hauled my furniture down one rickety set of stairs and up the next. Still angry about the robberies, I left the super a four-foot mound of trash in the living room, topped with a used tampon. Later, I was able to return Rita Mae's favor when she moved to DC, helping her shove her motorcycle into a U-Haul.

My new place was another immigrant tenement, like the one I was leaving, but here the landlord—a sad-faced guy in his forties—lived on the premises and kept an eye on things. Rosen, or perhaps the tenant before her, had painted each room a different color, and sometimes several colors. The light was good. There was an elementary school across the street, and the happy shouts of children drifted up during recess.

29

BACKPACK, MIC, AND TAMPONS

I'D JUST STARTED PRODUCING *Lesbian Nation* at WBAI when a student group at the University of Arizona invited me to speak. They were paying my airfare! I bought a one-way ticket, packed my mic and cassette recorder, and flew out. My plan was to use the other half of the money for a hitchhiking trip around the West.

I stepped off the plane into the Phoenix heat. I don't remember anything I said to the students that day, but I do remember that Richie Larsen, the guy who'd invited me, expressed some surprise at my tone. He'd heard my fire-breathing speech after being released from jail, after the Grove Press occupation two years earlier, and expected more of the same. But by 1972 I was in a more cheerful frame of mind.

Phoenix was the strangest place I'd ever seen, so different from the concrete canyons of NYC, or the lush, mosquito-ridden Catskills where I'd spent summers as a child. Mesquite trees. Big saguaro cacti, little prickly pears. Hordes of ants racing along the cracks in the sidewalks, faster than any ants back home. I wondered if the heat that slows us humans down supercharges ants.

Richie invited me to spend the night at a gay men's commune out in the countryside. We bounced over dirt roads, past what was instantly recognizable from the Looney Tunes cartoons as a roadrunner. It tore through the desert, revved up like the ants. Something else hovered in the sky just ahead of us, wings whirring like some gigantic bee. Richie told me it was a hummingbird. I had never seen one, but I have since learned that there are, in fact, ruby-throated hummingbirds in New York. They hang out in gardens with nectar-rich flowers—not the kind of place I would have visited during those frenetic years.

We arrived at a cabin about ten yards from the larger house where the landlord lived, and from the pen where he kept his pigs. Richie introduced me to the poor overcrowded beasts and then took me inside the cabin to meet the other members of the commune. One of them had some capsules of organic mescaline. The sun set, the temperature dropped, and soon we were all tripping in the moonlight, sitting on a patch of sand. Wisps of cloud morphed into a lace doily surrounding the full moon . . . it was all lovely except when the wind changed direction and suffused us with parfum de pigsty.

The next day I heard that one of the men had thrown himself off a nearby mountain and was in the hospital. Depression? Self-hate for being gay? Drug-induced hallucination? I never found out.

I told Richie that I wanted to go to Los Angeles and then Berkeley. He was between jobs at the time and decided to join me. Hitching together, we passed for a straight couple, which gave us a measure of safety. Our best ride was with two guys from rural Arkansas who were driving across the country. I could barely understand their Appalachian accents, but they were kind and friendly and took us the rest of the way to Los Angeles, where I met two of the artists who had created Womanhouse.

This feminist art installation had occupied an abandoned Victorian house in Hollywood for only one month, February 1972, but it drew national and international attention. Though Womanhouse had been dismantled by the time I arrived in Los Angeles, I was able to record the artists' descriptions, especially that of Judy Chicago's "menstruation bathroom." The shelves, I was told, were stocked with boxes of tampons and piles of sanitary napkins. Red rags hung on a small clothesline. Sitting below the shelves was a large trash can overflowing with what appeared to be used menstrual supplies. A tampon soaked in dried "blood" lay on the floor. Men who entered that room turned

Eva Blinder and I practice martial arts prior to one of my hitchhiking trips.

green around the gills and left immediately, much to the artists' amusement—and mine. As I edited that section of the tape, I spliced in a song from *Annie Get Your Gun*:

> *The girl that I marry will have to be*
> *As soft and as pink as a nursery.*
> *The girl I call my own*
> *Will wear satins and laces and smell of cologne . . .*

Later, still in L.A., I met up with a woman I'll call Diane. I had had an affair with her in New York. She had moved out west, gotten into primal scream therapy, and didn't want to resume the relationship. She suggested I try the therapy, but I wasn't interested. She also urged me to quit smoking. At the time I was disappointed—but in fact she had given me a gift.

After leaving Los Angeles, Richie and I hitched north. In Big Sur, remembering Diane's prodding me to quit, I ditched the cigarettes, and we hiked up and up along switchbacks for a twelve-hundred-foot elevation gain. I struggled through tobacco-saturated lungs to match Richie's pace, panting under the weight of a pack loaded with camping gear—and my mic, cassette recorder, and tapes. Two days later and twenty miles in, we arrived at Sykes Hot Springs, which we shared with two other backpackers. The springs were great. We'd soak and then whiz down a natural slide into a cold stream. Less delightful was a mountain of trash left by previous visitors. At least they had piled their rubbish in one area instead of dropping bits and pieces all over.

We had scored some of that organic mescaline back in Phoenix and spent a day tripping. Steller's jays—another species I'd never seen before—morphed into miniature peacocks, and pebbles in the stream became periwinkles.

When we hiked out, I was done with tobacco.

From there we hitched north again, to Berkeley, where Richie left me to return to Phoenix. I stayed for a few days, meeting with some of the local feminist poets. By then I was ready to go home, and by luck encountered Linda (not her real name), who was also from New York and heading back that way. Somewhat younger than I was and from a more affluent family, she owned a VW Beetle. We drove across the United States, sometimes on the highways, sometimes on back roads, stopping every now and then to wipe bug splat off the windshield. These days you could probably drive a thousand miles without needing to clean the window. We have wiped out vast numbers of insects and about one-third of the bird population.

The drive was uneventful except for when, having crossed into Canada, we reentered the United States at Niagara Falls. The Canadians gave us no trouble, but US Customs asked a lot of questions. I had had the foresight to hide my capsules of mescaline inside a Tampax tube, which I then resealed with glue, and tossed the box of tampons into the trunk of the car. I was wearing blue jeans, however, along with a fringed leather vest and leather hat, and looked like a prototypical hippie.

"Where did you two meet?" the male official asked.

"Berkeley," I replied, without thinking about it.

"Pull over to the side," he rasped.

They searched and searched. Linda knew I had drugs and was freaking out. "You can't do this to me. I'm going to call my father," she fumed at the customs agents. I was scared but sat quietly, hoping that if they found the mescaline I could get help from Emily Goodman, the attorney who'd represented us at the Grove Press occupation.

The female official was fishing around in the trunk. "I *know* they've got something." She sounded exasperated. "But I can't find it."

They let us go. I detested those officials, but I suppose I should be grateful they didn't plant anything in the car. And grateful for menstrual supplies as well—they had given me the material for a successful radio show and saved my ass from the feds.

30

A BRAWL ON A BOAT

"I'VE GOT TICKETS to the *Ms.* party tomorrow night, but I'm not going," Phyllis told me. "They're yours if you want them."

I did. It was July 1973 and the first anniversary of *Ms.* magazine. They had rented a Circle Line boat for the celebration. Phyllis Chesler was a big name in the feminist literary world—*Women and Madness* had been reviewed on the front page of the *New York Times* book review section—and she rated a pair of free tickets. My contributions to radical left and lesbian periodicals did not put me in that league, and my friend Connie wasn't a writer at all. However, I was always up for a party where I could meet other writers, while Connie was always up for a party.

The Circle Line operates a fleet of sightseeing boats that ply the city's waterways, including, of course, circling Manhattan. The boats hold up to five hundred people. Since the *Ms.* affair was scheduled at night, we wouldn't be gawking at any sights. Our boat would just cruise up and down the Hudson River for a few hours.

An attendant directed us to one of the large oval tables on the upper deck, with maybe a dozen people. Much to my delight an old friend, the playwright Myrna Lamb, was seated on my right, while another feminist—Vivian Gornick, in my hazy recollection—sat next to her. Connie was on my left. I didn't recognize any of the others dining with us.

The waiters served the usual rubber-chicken dinner with a bland white wine. They kept our glasses full. The one memorable course was the whole pineapple they brought out for dessert—memorable because the man sitting opposite us shoved it at Connie, along with the carving knife. "Here," he snapped. "You want to be a man? Cut the pineapple like a man!"

Connie had grown up in a tough neighborhood in Brooklyn, with a couple of brothers as large as she was, and had learned how to keep peace without taking shit. She replied mildly and proceeded to slice into the fruit. The man—probably in his early fifties and shorter and smaller than Connie—repeated his remark and elaborated on it. I jumped up and hurled the contents of my glass into his face.

The woman next to him (who was obviously his wife) screamed at me and Connie and perhaps at the other feminists as well: "You're nothing but a bunch of cunts!" Myrna stood up and said that since dinner was over, we should go elsewhere. The four of us walked away.

By then I had realized that the really important guests were the ad men and investors, and the writers were there only for decoration. However, we were stuck on the boat until it returned to the pier, so we decided we might as well enjoy the rest of the party. A section of the upper deck had been set aside as a dance floor, and an all-woman rock band was playing. Connie and I danced until the band took a short break.

As soon as the music stopped another man stepped out of the crowd. He was younger and taller than the guy at the table and had a drink in his hand. He stared down at me, his eyes shooting venom. "Why don't you go hang yourself!" he snarled. I suppose he picked on me because Connie was even taller than he was, and I seemed like a safe target. Later I learned that the man had been watching us for fifteen minutes, muttering obscenities, before he decided to accost me.

I stepped forward and shoved him in the chest, hard, with both hands. He must have been wearing leather-soled shoes. The deck was slippery metal, and there was a metal staircase right behind him. I hadn't noticed it. He went down backward, all the way to the bottom, and only saved himself from injury by grabbing the handrail. And probably by being slack-jointed with alcohol.

I was simultaneously relieved and disappointed—relieved that I would not be carted off to jail for assault or even manslaughter, but disappointed that he wasn't lying unconscious in a pool of his own blood.

Patricia Carbine, the managing editor of *Ms.*, was at my elbow immediately. She began chewing me out. I tried to tell her what he'd said, but she was having none of it. She said that if I wanted to fight with people I should wait until we were off the boat.

The next time I saw Phyllis Chesler, she said someone from *Ms.* had called her. She shouldn't have given her tickets to anyone else, and no one would be allowed to do so in the future. And I, Martha, was banned from their future events.

I actually didn't mind. The hatred that I'd experienced on that boat was hazardous to my health. Despite the Lavender Menace action, homophobia was still rampant in the women's movement. Too many women were terrified of being labeled "man-hating dykes" if they spoke up for their rights. We lesbians were expected to suck it up when men insulted us or our friends or lovers.

After that evening I swore that if I ever found myself at a party where straight men were present—men that I didn't know personally—I wouldn't drink. Not a drop. Happily, I've kept that vow.

At the Gay Pride march, 1973.

31

ESCAPE FROM NEW YORK

WHEN I WAS IN HIGH SCHOOL, my best friend repeated a sarcastic line about New Yorkers' provincialism: "The world ends west of the Hudson." At that time, I hadn't been west of the Hudson River and had no idea what the rest of the country was like. Ten years later, in February 1969, I visited the San Francisco Bay Area and resolved to move there. But the Stonewall Riots and subsequent gay activism distracted me from my plan. From 1969 to 1974 I was totally caught up in the Gay Liberation Front, the *Come Out!* and *RAT* newspapers, and then WBAI radio.

People seemed to like my show. The programming manager got no negative feedback from the audience, and neither did I—well, except for my mother. She told me that she always listened to the show and then added, "I don't agree with anything you say, but I love hearing your voice."

Most of the people I knew seemed comfortable with my new status as a media person. However, there were some odd incidents. While traveling around the West, recording interviews for WBAI, I let a friend use my apartment. She was barely twenty and couldn't afford her own place, so she had been living with an elderly relative in one of the outer boroughs—a stifling arrangement for a young lesbian. Upon my return, I found *fartha belly*, clearly meant as an insulting twist on my name, and a few more abusive remarks scrawled on the kitchen wall.

Judy Liebler, another adolescent, said she wanted to do a segment on my show, or even a whole show. I loaned her my cassette recorder and mic for a few days so she could prepare her contribution. She came back with a tape of her and another friend singing a childish ditty they'd made up about pubic hair. It was too late for me to create a decent program, so I went on the air and talked for a while. It was the worst show I ever did. In retrospect, I should have let the station engineer play music to fill the time slot.

Kate Millett, who suffered from bipolar disorder, invited me for dinner at her place and asked me to bring my recording equipment. She had me keep the cassette running while she rambled on in one of her manic phases, clearly convinced that every word she said was gold, and talked down to me as though I were a mere servant whose job it was to capture those precious nuggets. The tape was completely unusable. The lobster was delicious, though.

Though I didn't know it at the time, Liebler also had bipolar disorder. The difference in her biography and Millett's is striking. Millett's father was an abusive alcoholic who abandoned the family, but her mother seems to have been supportive. She excelled at school. When her family discovered that she was in love with another woman, a wealthy aunt paid to send her to Oxford for graduate study. I'm not sure why they thought a couple of years in England would "cure" her. She did marry a man at one time but continued to have women lovers. At age thirty-nine, she was diagnosed with mental illness, had several hospitalizations, and survived several suicide attempts. Yet despite this illness, she taught college and became an internationally famous author and activist. Her second marriage, to Sophie Keir, lasted until Millett's death at age eighty-three.

Liebler was very bright and creative but rejected by her family. When they found out that she was a lesbian, her mother refused to pay her college tuition unless she had a nose job. Presumably that would make her look less Jewish and more attractive to men. Unable to support herself economically, Liebler submitted to surgery. That "cure" didn't work either. (When my mother offered me a nose job for the same reason, I was already living independently and able to refuse.) Liebler's mental illness became apparent during late adolescence. Perhaps an early onset has a worse prognosis, or perhaps she didn't get any useful treatment. She committed suicide at age twenty-seven.

On the positive side, Pamela Barnes, who'd been attending Radicalesbians meetings, wanted to do some five-minute segments. She was from England and had a British sense of humor. The material she produced, using the name Mary Flowerpot, was very well received. However, she kept stretching her five minutes longer and longer each time and using up more of my half hour than I had planned.

Despite the show's popularity, I knew that I didn't want to make a career in radio. I wasn't sure what to do next. Writing has always been my passion. I'd kept up contact with Judy Grahn and the Oakland Women's Press Collective and was thrilled to find that they wanted to publish my first book of poetry, *Crossing the DMZ*. It came out in 1974.

Reading from my first poetry book, *Crossing the DMZ*, at a 1975 conference in Malibu. *Photo by Tee Corrine*

At the end of 1973 I turned thirty. Naturally I'd heard the expression, "Don't trust anyone over thirty." Now I too was over the hill! One day, walking on West Fourteenth Street, just to prove that I still had what it took, I reached up and grabbed one of those Walk–Don't Walk signs at an intersection and started to do pull-ups. The first went well. On the second, the sign broke away from its pole and came down on my head. I landed on the sidewalk, with broken glasses and the flesh on the bridge of my nose sliced and bleeding. I hurried away so as not to get arrested for destroying municipal property.

Back in my Lower East Side apartment, I washed the wound and slapped the slice back in place, with a Band-Aid covering it. It healed— but with a chunk of NYC soot underneath. It was an odd sort of birthday present. Some of the soot is still there and still visible. I carry a piece of my hometown with me, along with the accent, forever.

By 1974 I'd had brief affairs but no success in finding a long-term relationship. That spring the woman I'd had a most recent affair with dumped me for a man. I resolved some of my unhappiness in a risky and irresponsible way, as so many of us did when we were young: I hitchhiked to Chicago to stay with friends for a few days. My parents sent me the money to fly home.

Later that spring Margaret Stephendaughter arrived from Paris. I don't remember exactly how we met, but she stayed in my apartment for a week. She had been involved in the 1968 student uprisings in France and shared some hilarious feminist literature from that time. We made love every day. She insisted that the right way to live was in a collective house with other like-minded women. After that week she moved on to graduate studies in California.

Persuaded by Margaret's argument, and shortly after she left, I put together a collective. We rented a run-down house in Brooklyn. Within a couple of months two of the other women quit work and were spending their days in bed together. Apparently they expected me to come up with the rent. I left them behind and moved again, to a duplex in Staten Island that I shared with Eileen Kurtzman, her collie, and a litter of puppies that Eileen later found new homes for. The landlord lived downstairs—a nice man, he would give us produce from his garden. Staten Island was almost rural back then, before they built the Verrazano Bridge, and I loved taking the ferry into the city.

I didn't stay in Staten Island very long. Toward the end of summer, I called Judy Grahn and told her I was planning to move to the Bay Area. Much to my surprise—and delight—she said they had a room in their collective house.

I gave up my slot at the radio station and gave away all my furniture, except for the typewriter desk and chair, which I shipped to Oakland. My brother, Ira, helped me schlep sixty-pound boxes of books down the stairs and to the post office. Mom cried, saying she was sure she'd never see me again. (Unfortunately, she was right.)

A few friends, including Phyllis, gave me a farewell dinner. At the beginning of October I took the bus to the airport, suitcase and plane ticket in hand, feeling light-headed, as though I'd lost my ballast and come unmoored.

Leaving New York. Carrying a box of books to the post office.

One of the last things my mother said to me before I left was, "Get married, get married, get married!" I struggled for independence while she did her best to protect me from the hardships and dangers she'd overcome. She'd gone hungry as a child. She gave her children three meals plus vitamins. She'd married my father, a working stiff whom she was never in love with, because he was a citizen, and he did love her. Like millions of women all over the world, denied a decent education, given lower pay if they got work at all, and subject to male violence, she saw a husband as protection, and she encouraged me to marry up, saying, "It's just as easy to love a rich man as a poor man."

And I'd retort, "That means you don't love either one."

By the time I left New York, her kids were grown and out of the house, her disabled parents had died, and she'd gone back to work. The job she applied for—timekeeper at the local welfare center—required a high school diploma. Once again, she summoned the wellspring of bravado that brought her across the ocean. "I told them I completed high school in Havana but because of [the United States breaking relations with] the Castro regime, I couldn't get a copy of the diploma."

The Welfare Department accepted her explanation, and she was hired. Those years were happy ones for her.

32

CODE BLUE

I ARRIVED IN OAKLAND at the beginning of October 1974. The communal house on Terrace Street had two stories plus an attic. Each of the other women had a room on the second floor. Mine was in the attic.

My new housemates—two couples, Carol Wilson and Alice Molloy, Judy Grahn and Wendy Cadden—had their routines, and I tried to fit in. Carol said there were two rules: wash the dishes, and don't wash the dishes. That is, take a turn doing the cleanup, but don't do too much of it because we are making a feminist revolution and housework isn't all that high on the priority list. The cats' litter box was right at the entrance to the kitchen. Though otherwise somewhat on the slob side, I had a hard time with that.

I remember wandering around the neighborhood and walking north into a large park, through a grove of blue gum eucalyptus—a tree I hadn't noticed on my previous brief visits to the Bay Area. Vendors of eucalyptus oil have described its scent as bold, rich, and penetrating. On that first encounter it reminded me of cat pee.

We were all broke, putting everything into our political work. I had intended to devote myself to writing and to studying martial arts. My new housemates informed me, with a smile, that as a condition of living there—I was not paying rent—they expected me to work either with Carol and Alice at A Women's Place bookstore, or with Judy and Wendy at the Women's Press Collective (WPC). Maybe I could have located some other living situation that would allow me to persist in my original plans. However, without a network of friends encouraging me, and because I believed the WPC was one of the brightest flames in the feminist revolution, I opted to join the press.

The bookstore and the WPC were housed in a triangular building at the intersection of Broadway and College, about half a mile from the Terrace Street house. Judy, Wendy, five other women, and I were the press collective, which occupied a room behind the bookstore. Our equipment consisted of a little Multilith 1250 that printed one page at a time, a camera to make plates for the Multilith, a paper cutter, and collating tables. The WPC had also received a $500 grant from Glide Memorial Church and used it to buy an old Chief, which printed 17" × 22" sheets, i.e., four pages at a time.

During the first week of January, when I'd barely begun to settle in, the phone call came from New York. Mom had suffered a stroke and was in the hospital, unconscious. I was on the next plane.

When I arrived, a shrunken version of my mother lay under the blankets, and Dad was standing by the bed. A couple of years earlier, Mom had told me she'd been diagnosed with polymyalgia, an autoimmune disease. It gave her terrible headaches. I hadn't bothered to look it up. I was twenty-nine then, out in the world and having adventures. I had no interest in spending my life the way my mother did: being a housewife, raising her two girls, adopting her nephew, carrying bedpans for her disabled mother, looking after her blind father. I didn't want to hear about the miseries of old age, not then. So it wasn't until the actual event that my father shared what the doctors had told him: polymyalgia causes strokes.

They'd been treating Mom with prednisone. "That's what caused the moon face," Dad said, his voice matter of fact, his eyes brimming with love and agony.

A little while later Jeannette joined us, and then a doctor showed up. He told us the X-rays revealed that Mom's brain was more than half destroyed, and she would never recover. Dad couldn't accept it. He wanted to take her home and look after her, even as she was.

We came and went for the better part of a week. Sometimes I took Mom's hand, and she squeezed mine in return. The doctor dismissed it as just a reflex. He was wrong. However much diminished, she was still there. Now I too wanted to take her home and care for her.

One day at the end of the week Dad and I were standing in the hallway when we heard an alarm, and two people raced past us in hospital coats. They wouldn't let us into Mom's room while they were doing whatever they did in those days, trying to restart her heart. They weren't successful. When the doctor told us, Dad let out a short, high-pitched wail and then began to sob. I can still hear that wail, and it still breaks my heart.

33

WITH WRENCH IN HAND

I WORKED AT THE WOMEN'S PRESS COLLECTIVE from 1974 until 1977. The WPC was a flashlight battery of an operation powering a dynamo of social change. It gave voice to the genius of women, particularly lesbians, at a time when men owned almost all the print shops and publishing companies and would never let our work see the light of day. I'm thinking particularly of the poetry of Judy Grahn and Pat Parker, the art of Wendy Cadden and Karen Sjöholm, the linguistic analyses of Alice Molloy, and others too numerous to mention here. The press ran on volunteer and low-paid labor and donations from women with extra cash.

Other small women's presses, newspapers, and bookstores had been springing up around the country during the '70s. Judy and Wendy started the WPC in 1970, printing a collection of women's poetry and graphics on a mimeograph. Their work inspired women in Baltimore to open Diana Press in 1972.

We were riding a tide of radical feminism and, though we didn't realize it then, the high point of the post-WWII economy. The average worker's purchasing power had steadily increased, year after year, from 1947 to 1973. Then, in 1974, inflation outstripped wage increases, with a 5 percent loss in real income. The long downhill slide continued from there, through the Reagan years to the present day. But in the '70s, many of us could still work part time, live frugally, and pay the rent. We could devote most of the week to art and activism.

The Women's Press Collective. From left to right: Wendy Cadden, Anita Taylor-Oñang, Judy Grahn, me, Felicia Newme, and Willyce Kim. *Photo by Donna Gottschalk*

The WPC had published my first book of poetry, *Crossing the DMZ*, and was now in the process of producing an anthology, *Lesbians Speak Out*, which included one of my essays from the *Come Out!* newspaper. *Lesbians Speak Out* had 154 pages and was too big to be stapled. It needed to be perfect bound, meaning that the pages would be glued together into the spine. After typesetting, printing, trimming, and collating—all by hand—we had to clamp the pages together, one book at a time, smear the inside edges with hot glue, and slap the cover around them. We had just acquired a hot-glue machine for this project.

The hot-glue fumes were toxic, so we needed an exhaust fan to ventilate the room. I don't remember how it was that I volunteered, but one day I climbed a ladder outside the building. Perched on the ledge overlooking Broadway, I chiseled a hole in the stucco, and we plopped the fan in there. When I was done, Carol inspected the results and began to sing, "M-I-C-K-E-Y . . ." It was indeed a Mickey Mouse job, but it worked.

The WPC had a rule about how books were chosen for publication: two members had to agree on it. Since Judy and Wendy always voted the same way, and I seemed to be the only other person interested in reviewing submissions, their decisions held. Judy and Wendy chose works that promoted only the most positive images of women, which they believed was the best use of our limited resources. This made sense, given millennia of patriarchy and its depictions of women as stupid, weak, and passive.

On the other hand, at that time there was little space in the women's movement for some of the negative and painful aspects of life, or for those times when we and the people around us were less than heroic. When I was grieving my mother's death and wrote a short story about the depressed guy who'd been my landlord on the Lower East Side of Manhattan, their response was dismissive. After that I stopped writing for quite a while.

Although I did operate some of the simpler equipment at the WPC, I never learned to run a press. This wasn't for lack of ability, but lack of interest. I'd always been comfortable with basic tools—after all, hadn't I chiseled that hole in the wall of the building? A Polish woman I had done typing for also asked me to do little mechanical tasks in her apartment and observed, when I completed them, "You Americans are born with screwdrivers in your hands." But I didn't want to be a printer.

I felt very conflicted about accepting the few thousand dollars my mother left me, as I hadn't been the daughter she wanted. My younger sister filled that role—she lived with our parents throughout her college and graduate school years, opened a law practice, married a nice Jewish boy, had two children, and bought a house in the suburbs—while I was trying to organize the gay revolution.

In the long run I wasted much of the money, but did buy two useful items, a 1968 VW bug and a stereo set.

I had taken driving lessons in a VW before leaving New York. The driving school was just north of Greenwich Village, in an area with lots of commercial truck traffic. Too young and foolish to be nervous around those behemoths, I just followed instructions and got my license without difficulty.

When my small inheritance arrived, I decided to buy a VW bug. Someone steered me to Pat Davidson, feminist auto mechanic par excellence and one of the most honest people I've ever met. She had rebuilt the bug's engine after its first 120,000 miles. Pat was even shorter than I was, sturdy, with blonde hair and a ruddy complexion. She rented the basement garage of an apartment building for her business, Mole Hole Motors. "In three hundred miles you have to bring it back for an oil change," she advised. "I'll teach you how to do it if you like." Naturally I said yes.

Thus began a series of visits for oil changes, tune-ups, brake adjustments, brake shoe replacements, and (years later) a second engine rebuild. I acquired enough tools to fill the trunk of the car and two books—the official Volkswagen manual, and the Compleat Idiot repair book.

Me working on the VW bug.

One day I had been hiking at a regional park, thinking of my mother, and when I started the engine to drive home the tears blinded me. Trying to pull out of the parking lot, I slammed into a foot-high concrete post and bent the front axle. The car was still drivable, but just barely. We made it to Mole Hole. Pat and I jacked up the front end and removed the wheels. Pat then lay on her back beneath the car and held the new axle in place with her feet, serving as a human jack, while I tightened the bolts.

34

A DREAM OF FLYING

I WAS VERY MUCH A NOVICE DRIVER. I remember taking three members of the Women's Press Collective across the Bay Bridge in my new car and thinking that if I made a mistake I'd wipe out our entire enterprise. All the same, despite my lack of behind-the-wheel experience, I decided to take the next step and learn to pilot a plane.

This wasn't an entirely new idea. At age ten I had dreamed of going to Mars. Frequent visits to the Hayden Planetarium and liberal doses of science fiction had kept that ambition alive. As a young teenager I believed that you had to be a pilot to join the space program, but I didn't have the money for lessons, nor did I know of an aviation school in New York.

When I was fifteen, an Air Force recruiter came to our high school. He sat at a desk in one of the halls. About twenty feet away a small group of girls in ill-fitting blue skirts marched back and forth, broomsticks over their shoulders. *Hup, two, three, four . . .* If that was what it took to get into space, I'd put up with it.

"You'll teach me how to fly," I said confidently.

The arrogant twerp replied, "We don't teach girls to fly."

"Well, what do you teach girls to do?"

"Be a secretary or a weather girl."

I didn't need the military to teach me how to be a secretary. I walked off.

It wasn't until 1973 that an American commercial airline hired their first woman pilot, Bonnie Tiburzi. She was twenty-four and had connections—she learned the trade at her daddy's knee, as he had flown for SAS and TWA. That same year, the navy began allowing women to train as pilots.

In 1975, I was a longtime antiwar activist, anarcho-socialist, and lesbian feminist, and I had no intention of joining NASA, the Air Force, or any other government agency, even if there had been the remotest chance that they would accept me. Instead, I came up with the notion of starting my own company, Amelia Airlines, where women would hold all the jobs, from pilot to mechanic to flight attendant.

The nearest aviation school was in Hayward. My instructor was the epitome of niceness and competence, and he seemed to have no problems with female students. The first lesson was something of a disappointment, though. I had fantasized that piloting a small plane would feel like those dreams of flying, with the wind in my hair. Instead, we rode up and down in a small, noisy box—so noisy I could barely understand the radio communications from the control tower.

Nevertheless I persisted, at least for a while. One day I managed to put the plane in a nose dive, inadvertently simulating zero gravity, with papers flying around the cockpit. My instructor rescued us from what would have been a lethal crash. I thought it was funny, but when I told the story to my housemates, they were not amused.

A lesson or two later, I asked the instructor how long it would take to get a commercial pilot's license and how much would it cost. He said it would be at least $30,000 ($163,000 in today's dollars), many times the amount I had. At that point I gave up on aviation.

Shortly after that, and as a result of the Inez Garcia trial, I learned to operate a smaller piece of hardware: a Firestar 9 mm semiautomatic pistol.

35

MARTHA GOT HER GUNS

I NEVER THOUGHT ABOUT FIREARMS before I moved to Oakland in October 1974. Growing up in New York City, I never saw a pistol except on the hip of a cop, or a rifle except in the hands of an agent provocateur who tried to entrap me. For all my revolutionary talk, I had never handled a gun.

During the 1960s and '70s, various radical groups distributed posters of Third World women fighting for freedom in their countries. Those women were pictured with rifles or even AK-47s, bandoliers stuffed with cartridges over their shoulders, and babies on their backs. Now it seems absurd to believe that a nursing mother would haul her infant into battle or would even pick up a gun unless enemies were about to invade her home.

The Inez Garcia case kindled my interest in actually owning and using firearms. For those who don't remember, Garcia was a farmworker who in March 1974 shot and killed one of the men who raped her. While championing Garcia I began to feel like a hypocrite. I decided to learn to shoot.

After some research and experimentation, I acquired a .38 special, a 9 mm semiautomatic, and a 30-30 deer hunting rifle—though I had no intention of hurting anything with fur or feathers. Various friends offered instruction, including Carol Wilson, who showed me how to use the rifle. By that time I had moved out of the collective house where I was living and rented my own apartment near Lake Merritt.

My first opportunity to use a gun arose when Pamela Barnes, who had worked with me at WBAI-FM, flew out to visit. After a short stay in the Lake Merritt apartment, she started an affair with Suzanne, another woman in the feminist community, and moved in with her. One night, when they had gone camping together near Santa Rosa, two men raped them at gunpoint. Suzanne wanted to forget the whole thing, dismissing it as just another incident of bad sex with a man. Pamela came to me, distraught. She had been forced to suck off one guy and couldn't stop vomiting.

I was enraged. Pamela and I devised a plan. During the rape, to protect herself she had pretended to enjoy the experience and want more, so she had gotten his name and address. We decided to kidnap him at gunpoint, tie him naked to a tree, and paint his dick blue. We would tack a sheet of paper to the tree describing his crimes. I packed my 9 mm and five of us—Louise Merrill, Judy Grahn, Wendy Cadden, Pamela, and I— drove to the address Pamela had been given. When we arrived, however, there was no sign of him, and a neighbor said he had left the area.

The second opportunity came when a woman who wanted to join our community picked up her toddler, left her husband, and found a place to stay. If I remember correctly, she was from a Mormon family and had decided to come out as a lesbian. She was afraid her husband might come after her, so I went over there that evening, pistol in hand, thinking to provide protection. The gun scared her so much that she went back into the closet.

Not long afterward, Carol became involved with a woman named Diane. She helped Diane secure the apartment adjacent to mine, and Diane agreed to feed my cat when I went away for few days. I returned to find all my weaponry gone. As I was surveying the damage, my phone rang. When I picked up, a man's voice said, "Hey Diane! Got anything more for me?" It turned out that Diane was a heroin addict. Carol had known that, but she thought that love and trust would cure her. I was really pissed, to say the least.

My third opportunity occurred after I had acquired another 9 mm. There were stories in the news about a man stalking women in Oakland

and raping them at knifepoint. We were urged to stay at home until he had been caught. *I'm not going to be kept prisoner*, I thought. *If he has a knife, I have a gun.* I put the gun in a holster designed to look like a fanny pack and went hiking in one of the regional parks.

It was no fun. Instead of being able to enjoy a peaceful hike, I felt like a soldier in enemy territory, expecting an attacker behind every tree. And then what? If I wanted to get the drop on the rapist, I'd have to be walking around with the gun in my hand. I couldn't ask him to wait while I unsnapped the pack, drew, and aimed.

The men who raped Inez Garcia called her home afterward and threatened to kill her if she didn't leave town. Instead, she took her son's .22 rifle and went after them, killing one.

She was charged with murder. Her attorney, famed radical Charles Garry, tried to get her acquitted on diminished capacity, arguing that she was cognitively impaired and didn't know what she was doing. Garcia was having none of it. She shouted at the judge, "I killed the son of a bitch because I was raped! And I'd kill him again!"

The judge instructed the jury that whether she was raped was irrelevant. Garcia was convicted of second-degree murder and sentenced to five years. Afterward, a male juror commented, "A rapist is just trying to give her a good time."

The women's movement was outraged. Feminists thought Charles Garry's diminished-capacity strategy came out of his own patriarchal, patronizing attitudes. We demonstrated, raised funds, and hired attorney Susan Jordan, who eventually obtained a new trial, claiming self-defense. Garcia was acquitted and released in 1977.

Many years later I still owned that 9 mm when I moved in with a woman who had a troubled twelve-year-old boy. She was afraid that no matter how well I hid the gun, he would find it, and someone would get killed. I got rid of it. (She was prescient, because when he later started using drugs he attacked her, and I had to fight him off. It wasn't too hard—he believed that I was a terrific martial artist and was afraid that I would hurt him.)

With rare exceptions, perhaps including the Garcia case, guns do not make women safer. According to the *Guardian*, around fifty-seven American women are murdered every month by an intimate partner. "The gun control advocacy group Everytown estimates that in 57% of the mass shootings that occurred between January 2009 and June 2014, the perpetrator killed an intimate partner or family member. . . . A woman in an abusive relationship is five times more likely to be killed by her partner if there is a gun in the house. It doesn't matter if the gun belongs to her or to him: the presence of any weapon in a home afflicted with domestic violence means that the abuser is more likely to use it to kill her." Not included in the statistics are the multitudes who survive gunshot wounds with lasting damage, both physical and psychological.

I don't have an answer to male violence, which has gone on for millennia. Still, I am sure that the casualty level would be drastically reduced if men—and women—weren't allowed to own guns. Yes, I'm talking about *confiscation*. Of course, men will scream about their Second Amendment rights, but what they're really talking about, and what none of the discussions in the media will come near, is *castration*. I think about US Marine recruits parading with their rifles and chanting, "This is my rifle, this is my gun, this is for fighting, this is for fun." They seize their crotches at "gun" and "fun."

36

IN PRINT AND
ON THE ROAD

A DAY'S WORK AT THE WOMEN'S PRESS COLLECTIVE might include any of the following: typesetting, printing, collating, binding, or packing books for shipping to stores and individual purchasers. Running the press required a higher level of skill than the other tasks, but most of what we did was repetitive hand labor, and it was actually quite pleasant. Since we didn't have a collating machine, we'd walk around a big table laying pages out by hand, talking about this and that.

To get customers, we also needed to market, which meant going to bookstores and feminist events and doing readings. Sometimes we attended gatherings just to meet other feminists and have a good time.

A Winter Solstice Celebration

Judy Grahn and I participated in the 1975 winter solstice celebration in Los Angeles, which was organized by Zsuzsanna (called Z) Budapest. Z had founded the women-only Dianic Wiccan coven there. Upon arriving in L.A., I was surprised to discover that an old friend from New York, Kathryn McHargue, had moved there and become Z's lover. Kathryn didn't seem happy. She had always struck me as an introvert who needed one lover to focus on her and care for her. Z was wildly extroverted and demanded the attention of many people. The relationship wouldn't last.

The solstice celebration took place on the side of a nearby mountain. We stripped to the waist, drank whiskey laced with cayenne to keep warm, and danced around the fire. Then we were supposed to hug and kiss the other women in the circle. Judy remembers me kissing Z, open-mouthed and erotic. I have no memory of doing that, and to me it seems very unlikely, but I do remember landing such a kiss on another woman in the group. I'm not going to tell who, though.

The following night, a member of the coven asked Z how to tell the difference between a waxing and a waning moon. Z waved her fingers at the sky, a gesture that was both airy and authoritative, and replied that a waning moon looks crumbly, like a cookie that someone has chewed on. I was astonished by their ignorance but shouldn't have been. More than 70 percent of Americans are scientifically illiterate, and about 20 percent believe the sun revolves around the earth.

Even more distressing, though, was Z's willingness to make up such nonsense and foist it on her credulous followers.

The Women in Print Conference

The first Women in Print Conference took place at the end of August, in 1976, on land rented from the Campfire Girls outside of Omaha, Nebraska. Some Women's Press Collective members attended. I drove out in my beloved VW bug. It was a joyous time: summer heat, the Platte River, a big swimming pool, a zillion grasshoppers. We made connections with other small presses and bookstores and exchanged ideas about how to better publish and distribute our materials. I don't remember much of what we said, except for an idea from Nancy Stockwell, who wrote for *Plexus*, a feminist newspaper out of Berkeley. She speculated that brown grasshopper spit could be harvested and turned into print ink.

Most important was the realization that our projects weren't going to be financially successful or even survive long term. As Charlotte Bunch said in an interview in *Sinister Wisdom*:

It's funny that in 1976, after years with women's liberation ideology in which we learned that the society oppressed us, in which we learned that society was a capitalist patriarchy, that big business and multinational corporations control, that small businesses were, in fact, on the way out, we nonetheless all still felt that if we just worked harder, if we just did it better, our projects would survive. Some of that mythology broke down at the Women in Print Conference because when we sat down and talked about some of the problems in getting out a journal—things like the fact that no matter what price you set your journal at, even though you kept thinking it cost too much, you still couldn't make it financially—we learned that no publication survived solely on selling its product—that they're all either subsidized by major corporations or they're subsidized by universities or they're publications of organizations whose membership subsidizes them. We had a lot to learn about publishing in America.

At a conference with women from small feminist presses and bookstores.

The Press Collective was subsidized by both unpaid and greatly underpaid labor. We also received donations from well-to-do feminists who believed in our work. Diana Press of Baltimore took in commercial print jobs so they could publish women's literature. Even the major patriarchal news outlets, like the *New York Times*, required massive infusions of advertising revenue.

I was, in fact, aware of the economic constraints on our industry but hadn't begun to imagine a solution. Perhaps I expected we could somehow manage to continue in the same way, living on poetry and revolutionary fervor.

A day or so before leaving the conference, one of the women discovered wild marijuana growing along the Platte River. We harvested bags of it, and I stuffed some into the trunk of my bug. It hadn't gone to flower, though, and upon reaching home I discovered that a joint of it had as much potency as toilet paper.

37

NARROW ESCAPES

In February 1977 I received a call from Pamela. After living with Suzanne for some months, she had decided to make the Bay Area her home and needed to clear out her apartment in Manhattan. Would I travel with her to NYC and help her move? I said yes, thinking a cross-country trip would be fun—a grand adventure, and an opportunity to visit old friends and family back east.

Suzanne, who earned part of her living dealing pot and psychedelics, let us have a few ounces of marijuana at wholesale so we could sell it to finance the trip. I thought we could also sell Press Collective books, thus making money and promoting the cause at the same time.

One evening, shortly before we left, I went to Max Dashu's place. My visit had something to do with preparing for the drive from the Bay Area to New York, with getting assistance or information from one of Max's housemates. Max—whom I'd never met before—listened quietly during a long conversation about the proposed trip. When the housemates and I were done talking, Max turned to me and asked, "Why don't you come upstairs and get to know me better?"

I followed her to her bedroom. The walls were covered with brightly colored art, some prints and some Max's own drawings. I was impressed. She put on music, and we danced and then went to bed. I hadn't expected to start a new relationship just before leaving town, but there it was. We saw each other a few more times, and I told her I'd be in touch when someone let me use her phone for a long-distance call. (For you younger readers: This was before mobile phones. There were only landlines.)

Departure day arrived. This would be Pamela's second big move, the first being from her native England. She had purchased a used car, a big boat of a sedan. We loaded the trunk with our sleeping bags, some changes of clothes, the bags of marijuana that we got from Suzanne, and books from the Women's Press Collective—anthologies like *Lesbians Speak Out*, some lesbian poetry collections including my own *Crossing the DMZ*, and *The Women's Gun Pamphlet*. And then we were on the road.

In those days you could show up at any women's center in the United States, and whoever was running the place would welcome you and let you sleep on the couch or the floor. I figured we could go from one city to the next, selling feminist literature and pot while avoiding motel bills. I was also planning to do fundraising for the Women's Press Collective.

Reno was our first stop, and that's where things started to go downhill. We drove to what was supposed to be the local women's center, hoping to spend the night, and found out that the director wanted us to register. She kept a log of visitors and shared it with the police. Pamela suggested that we sign false names. I refused. We slept in the car that night. It was pretty cold, at forty-five-hundred-foot altitude in February. In retrospect Pamela may have been right, and perhaps I was more self-righteous than sensible.

In Salt Lake City we connected with an instructor at one of the universities, a lone feminist in a sea of patriarchal Mormonism. She was separated from her husband, and I got the impression that an actual divorce would have cost her her job. She put us up for the night in a spare bedroom. We both liked her.

At the women's center in Denver, we met someone who used the alias Woodwoman. Originally from South Africa, Woodwoman was Jewish, a lesbian, a Communist, and a supporter of the African National Congress. She had left the country one step ahead of the apartheid police. She didn't say how she'd entered the United States but did let us know that she wasn't in the country legally. At home in South Africa she had read my article "Notes of a Radical Lesbian" in *Sisterhood Is Powerful* and had come to understand that her sexuality wasn't just an incidental or private matter, but was as political as her race and sex. I was enormously gratified to learn that something I wrote had traveled halfway around the world and affected another woman's life.

Somewhere in Iowa we encountered a snowstorm. I was behind the wheel. The car skidded on the ice and spun around, stopping at a ninety-degree angle to the road. I threw the doors open and flipped on the overhead lights. The oncoming driver slammed on the brakes and stopped without hitting us. It was a scare, but I felt good about the way I'd handled it. We slept at the center in Iowa City. The women there were connected with the university and, like many feminists at that time, wore denim overalls. They were delighted to get their hands on literature from the WPC.

By this time Pamela was really angry with me. "I was supposed to be the star of this trip," she said. "Not you." I was astonished. What was she expecting? Perhaps that I would be a combination of social secretary, relief driver, and presenter of Pamela as a celebrity? She wasn't known as a writer, artist, or organizer. She wasn't even a member of any feminist organization. I had been getting us free housing by using my credentials as a writer and WPC member. Other women were paying attention to me because of those credentials and because of the books I'd brought to share with them.

In NYC, while Pamela closed down her apartment, I stayed with friends for a few days, and from there I was able to call Max and tell her we had arrived safely. I continued to peddle our wares. Audre Lorde bought an ounce of marijuana. Later she called to say that it was wretched stuff and didn't even give her a buzz. I had no idea, as I'd never tried any of the weed Suzanne had given us. I refunded the money, feeling terrible. Was it all crap dope that Suzanne wanted us to unload on people across the country, people who couldn't come after her? How many women had I sold it to?

By now it was March and time to head home. Pamela had recruited a man I'll call Jimmy, a volunteer programmer from WBAI who wanted to go to California and was willing to share expenses. I don't remember him doing any of the driving, as he was a native New Yorker and probably never had a license. Pamela drove the whole way. She wouldn't let me behind the wheel and barely spoke to me during the rest of the trip. When she did, it was with contempt. Jimmy took his cues from her. I was miserable and began to hate them.

We took the southern route. I don't remember where we slept, except that we holed up in a motel in Mississippi during a tornado watch. The trek across Texas was interminable. Pamela sped up and was doing 80 mph when the highway patrol pulled us over.

I was sweating. If the cop searched the car we were done for. Texas was—and still is—giving people life sentences for drug possession, even for the smallest amounts. Possession of lesbian literature and copies of *The Women's Gun Pamphlet* wouldn't have impressed a judge favorably either. Pamela, however, sweetly apologized for speeding, pretending to be an ignorant foreigner. Her British accent and blonde hair must have made the right impression. The cop was equally polite, escorting us to the courthouse where Pamela paid a fine and they let us go. Pamela gloated over her triumph. After that, though, she kept to the speed limit.

In Tucson, where my old friend Mary McCarthy lived, I told Pamela to let me off. Mary put me up for the night and drove me to the highway in the morning. I started hitchhiking. By evening I reached Bakersfield, unrolled my sleeping bag in a vineyard, and slept in the furrows. At first light I was up and out before the farmworkers arrived.

From there it was half a day's ride home. Angry, exhausted, and traumatized, I never spoke to Pamela or Suzanne again. However, I had sold most of the books and at least half of the weed, had obtained pledges of $9,000 for the WPC, and was looking forward to exploring my new relationship with Max.

Shortly after my arrival, I found that Judy and Wendy had been persuaded into another, more ambitious plan for keeping the press collective running.

38

A DREAM COMES UNDONE

IN THE SPRING OF 1977, after that disastrous trip with Pamela, I took to bed with a fever from some microbe I had picked up. I was looking forward to resuming work at the Women's Press Collective and seeing Max again. But my world was about to be overturned.

Judy Grahn came to visit during my recuperation, bringing some roast chicken—rather a surprise, as this was unusual behavior for her. Then she told me about the new plan to keep the WPC running and even make it profitable, instead of depending on donations and volunteer labor. We would join a consortium, the Feminist Economic Network (FEN), but this required restructuring our operation.

FEN had originally been organized in 1975 in Detroit. By 1977 it was composed of Diana Press, the Detroit Federal Feminist Credit Union, and the Oakland Feminist Women's Health Center (for brevity, the Credit Union and the Health Center). The planned merger meant that the WPC would have access to Diana's better equipment and receive job training.

During her visit, Judy explained that our new structure would be based on the Health Center's, meaning that two individuals would be the directors—in our case, Judy and her lover, Wendy—and the rest of us would be employees. I was hurt and angry. We were supposedly a collective, even if some members tended to assume more power than others. If I had wanted to be an employee, I would have gotten a straight job, with better pay.

At that time, I knew very little about FEN or about the Health Center. In November, before leaving on that trip with Pamela, I had signed a leaflet deploring attacks on those entities, without really knowing anything about the circumstances. After returning to the Bay Area and recovering from my illness, I started asking questions. I interviewed many women who had experience with the Health Center, including Laura Brown, one of the directors, and some of the doctors as well.

The Health Center

The Health Center was a nonprofit, set up in 1972 by Laura Brown and Debra Law, who were then the directors. Later Barbara Hoke became Brown's lover and another director. Below them were employees and contract workers. Newly hired employees had to give a year's commitment, not be in therapy, not be in school, and not be a socialist. The workweek was sixty hours, six days a week. Base pay was $88 a week for trainees and $110 for staff. Sometimes, however, the workers got only 50 to 70 percent of that, depending on the finances of the center, and sometimes they didn't get paid at all. To put it in context, the median wage for health care workers in the 1970s was $120 to $205 for a forty-hour week. Staff members had to attend meetings, during which the employees who were not in favor at the time were publicly shamed and often reduced to tears. Turnover was very high.

Women who had tried to do the accounting for the Health Center said that the books were a mess. One showed me a financial statement listing over $30,000 for overhead, but neither rent nor phone was included. She couldn't figure out where the money had gone. She said that patients were encouraged to pay in cash, and the cash box was in the care of a staff member with a heroin habit, so some of the money may have been diverted that way. The Health Center also paid Brown and Hoke to travel around the country giving speeches and doing self-help demonstrations.

Most reports were that the Health Center's care was good for general GYN, birth control clinics, Pap smears, and self-help classes. Abortions were reasonably priced for the time at $185. The staff members I interviewed thought that abortion care was done according to medical standards. However, counseling took place in groups rather than individually. Patients were not allowed to bring anyone in for support, including their partners. They weren't allowed to talk directly with the doctors (all male), who were treated as technicians, presumably to put power in the hands of the women running the clinic. If a patient asked a question, one of the counselors would reply. Of most concern, however, women were denied pain medication during abortions.

Why? Apparently the directors gave the clinic staff different reasons at different times. One staff member was informed that women who used painkillers lay on the table longer and were in aftercare longer, and time is money. Another was advised that Valium (which was supplied only if a woman was nervous) cost too much, at 60¢ per pill. I checked this out myself at a local pharmacy and found that Valium actually retailed at 8.5¢ a pill. Even 60¢ would not have been such a big bite out of the $185 total—give me a break!

The patients themselves were told that it was a sign of weakness to take painkillers during an abortion, that it was more "feminist" to bear the pain. A supporter of the center reported to me that the policy was to make abortions difficult, because they didn't want to be patching up the messes left by men. They wanted to give women incentives to *not* come back. Supposedly this was a radical idea. I couldn't, and still can't, see how it is feminist or radical to punish women for having sex. And some of the pregnancies must have been the result of rape.

———————

I was recently forwarded an old article about the Health Center, published May 1973 in the *Argus*, a Fremont, California, newspaper. It quoted Laura Brown at length; she stated that the Health Center charged only $150 for an abortion while Bay Area hospitals had been charging $800 to $1,000. She said that once feminists announced their plan to provide the service at a reduced rate, some of those hospitals lowered their prices to match. If that were the case, the Health Center would have deserved kudos.

However, after thinking it over, I find it hard to believe that such a small operation could have had such a large effect just by announcing its abortion fees. Even at the time the article was published, the Health Center had performed no more than five abortions.

Roe v. Wade had been decided in January 1973. At the end of the year the *New York Times* reported that first trimester abortions cost $150 at the clinics they surveyed in Pittsburgh and in Detroit. The average cost in hospitals was $350. It seems unlikely that facilities around the nation based their prices on a decision made by one little clinic in Oakland.

To put things in perspective, with inflation, $150 in 1973 is equivalent to about $1,000 today. That would have been a considerable sum for a person without health insurance.

39

THE DEBACLE
IN DETROIT

DEEPLY DISTURBED BY WHAT I had learned about the Health Center, I took
the train to Detroit, where the Feminist Economic Network was based,
to make inquiries there. The responses I got from the women involved
were overwhelmingly, though not completely, negative.

The Detroit Feminist Federal Credit Union

The Detroit Feminist Federal Credit Union was started by Joanne
Parrent and Valerie Angers in 1973. Credit unions work somewhat
like banks but are not-for-profit and designed to be governed by their
members. In 1974, Parrent and Angers traveled to Oakland and met
with Brown and Hoke at the Health Center, where the four of them
conceived the idea of FEN. In November 1975 this new entity was born.
Among the bylaws were: 1) FEN will accept financial leadership for the
women's movement. (I'm not sure who was supposed to have offered
it to them.) 2) Decision-making power will be confined to the board
of directors, who shall be founders of, and working for three years in,
a self-supporting feminist enterprise.

Apparently the initial board consisted of three couples: Brown and
Hoke of the Health Center, Parrent and Angers of the Credit Union,

and Casey Czarnik and Coletta Reid of Diana Press. They established a holding company, the FEN Association, to own and control all subsidiaries and, as their articles of incorporation put it, "to buy assets and property of every kind." They attempted to set up branches of the Credit Union in thirteen Midwestern states but weren't able to get a charter. If they had succeeded, they would have been able to draw on the assets of those branches via computer, without any real control by the members, who likely would not have had the resources or time to travel to meetings in Detroit.

What they did instead was to draw assets where they could. The Credit Union borrowed $200,000 from the Michigan Credit Union League (MCUL), a nonprofit organization that provided support to community credit unions. The Detroit Feminist Federal Credit Union then loaned eight women $32,000 each, for a total of $256,000. None of these women were eligible for such large sums—one, in fact, was living on welfare. The women then turned the money over to FEN. In this way the FEN Corporation circumvented the law prohibiting credit unions from lending to corporations. FEN then used the money to buy a six-story building that had housed the Detroit Women's City Club and to refurbish it with new furniture, chandeliers, and other decor.

Having given the money to FEN, the eight women weren't able to pay back the loans, so the Credit Union was required to reimburse the MCUL. Making good on the defaulted loans tied up all the savings of Credit Union members. No one could access her own money or obtain a loan, large or small.

The FEN directors hired a crew of women to prepare their newly acquired building for the grand opening. They worked the crew long hours and fired those who couldn't meet their demands. FEN then tried to rook the women out of their wages entirely, but one woman called the state employment department, which forced FEN to write checks. Even so, some of the workers did not get paid for all the hours they put in.

The building was supposed to house various businesses, hotel rooms, and a new Feminist Women's Health Center. Such a center already existed in Detroit, but the director—a White woman—had fallen out of favor. Brown set up a rival center. She trained three Black women over a long weekend. These three were among the eight who had signed for the $32,000 loans that FEN used to buy the building. One of them later told me they had been promised autonomy in running the center but that, in actuality, business decisions were made by the FEN directors.

At that point, I was told, FEN began to fall apart. Laura Brown started a secret affair with Joanne Parrent. Parrent's partner Valerie Angers, an interior decorator, was asked to prepare the best suite in the building in anticipation of a visit from a high-ranking federal official. Once she had put in a fourteen-hour day painting and decorating the rooms, Brown and Parrent moved into the suite, and it became their love nest. Brown's partner Hoke didn't seem to mind, but Angers was beside herself with fury. She tipped off the National Credit Union Administration about the illegal financial transactions. The others isolated her from the rest of the staff and castigated her for putting her personal feelings above the goals of the revolution.

When members came to demand that the building be returned to the Credit Union—and sold, I guess, in order to pay back the loans—the FEN board called on their security guards. A fight broke out, and some women were punched and kicked, but none badly hurt. The FEN women called the police, who evicted the protestors. This incident was reported in the local press.

FEN collapsed economically. Brown filed a petition with the court to dissolve the corporation. A net debt of around $80,000 had to be paid off. I don't know whether that figure included $15,000 in taxes owed to the IRS. A woman named Kay, who owned a boutique in the building, said she bought some of the furniture for $11,500. The FEN directors took the rest of the furniture, whatever they could cram into U-Haul trucks, and fled to Oakland.

That was when Laura Brown and her associates approached Judy and Wendy. As I understand it, the plan was to reconstitute FEN, now with the inclusion of the WPC. Other targets for acquisition were Olivia Records, *Chrysalis* magazine, and the Los Angeles Women's Building.

What I Did with the Research

Based on my interviews, I wrote a twenty-two-page article that included an impassioned (and admittedly overwrought) three-page analysis. I mailed it around the country, and it was published in the Denver feminist newspaper *Big Mama Rag*.

Because of my anger, I didn't tell Judy and Wendy about my findings before publishing, but just sprung it on them. The therapist I had been seeing to deal with the anguish around my mother's sudden death said that was a mistake. She was right. Those relationships were severely damaged, and we didn't speak to each other for decades. Fortunately, the three of us have now lived long enough to become good friends again, though we will never agree on the issues that divided us back in 1977. Had I presented the information to them at the time, before publication, it likely wouldn't have changed their minds about a merger with FEN, but it would have caused less pain.

The Aftermath

The WPC split apart, with one side not talking to the other. Judy accused me of speaking only to the anti-FEN people for my article and not to Laura Brown. In fact, I had interviewed Brown, but I didn't find her account of events to be at all plausible.

I stayed around the offices of the WPC just long enough to finish production of Alice Molloy's new book, *In Other Words*. By then FEN had ceased to exist. Meanwhile, during that period, Judy invited Diana Press to move to Oakland, where it merged with the WPC. Judy reports in her memoir that this worked until the fall of 1977, despite attacks by unknown perpetrators that included sabotaging their phones and slashing tires. Someone broke in and destroyed the printing equipment. They must have known what they were doing, because the damage was quite thorough. Was it the FBI? Feminist or Marxist dissidents? Right-wingers? No one ever identified the attackers.

What was left of the joint venture lasted for another year, and then it folded.

Laura Brown blamed the debacle in Detroit and the criticism of the Health Center on racism and classism from White middle-class women who were "downwardly mobile." In her opinion, FEN was antiracist and working class. The women of color that I interviewed all disagreed—every one of them described the FEN operations as either structurally racist, with all the decisions being made by White women at the top, or at the very least culturally insensitive.

———————

Perhaps we all believe what fits into our worldview and our needs at a given time. I am a socialist of sorts, though not a doctrinaire one, and have even described myself at times as an anarcho-communist—someone who would never have been hired at the Health Center. In her memoir, Judy said my article implied that she and Wendy were Laura's puppets. That certainly wasn't my intention. I perceived them as being exhausted, tired of being poor, and tired of living on donations while doing important work. Though I believe they were mistaken, FEN seemed to offer them a way to be properly recompensed for their contributions to the feminist movement.

Judy writes that FEN, as an economic powerhouse, if it had continued, would have been of benefit to all women. I'm dubious. My late friend and political mentor Marion Youers always said the question is whether you believe that the ends justify the means, or that the means shape the ends. I think the latter.

Judy's interpretation of these events is in her memoir and is radically different from what I have written here. I know that her perceptions and judgment about what happened are sincere. As for me, my belief in my research and conclusions is firm. She and I will never see eye to eye on what happened and who was responsible. I'm hoping that we can agree to disagree and continue our friendship, which is enormously valuable to me, especially as we grow older and have limited time.

Back in 1977 I was devastated by the loss of the comradeship that the WPC had offered me and of the friendships that had meant so much to me. It was one of the worst periods of my life.

Max and I continued to see each other, and she was supportive during this period. Soon after I was done with Alice's book and left the WPC, she suggested another road trip. This seemed to promise a good distraction while I figured out what to do with the next phase of my life. So I tuned up the VW bug and off we went.

40

WITH MAX IN THE
RED BEETLE

Max Dashu was somewhat taller than I was, with short blonde hair, a high forehead, and square features. She came from a small town in the Midwest. Her father died when she was a teenager, leaving her mother to raise five children in poverty. Exceptionally bright and wanting to get out into the wider world, she got her chance with a full scholarship to Harvard. She didn't fit in there, though, either socially or intellectually. Her classmates were privileged young women with cashmere sweaters and, as she saw it, the instruction was all about teaching people what to think, and Harvard itself existed to facilitate connections among the young elite. She dropped out and struggled to survive while doing independent research in the subject of her passion, women's history.

In the summer of 1978, Max and I made ready for our road trip. Max wanted to visit museums with collections of Native American art, specifically art made by women, and take photos for the slideshows that, years later, would become her internationally known Women's History Archives. I had no idea what to do next. Perhaps a cross-country journey would be a salve to my wounds.

For those who have never looked under the hood of a VW Beetle, that's where the trunk is, where you put your luggage or groceries or whatever. Behind the passenger compartment, in the space that in most cars would be the trunk, is the engine. Since I stored my tools in the trunk, we took the back seats out of the bug and packed in tents, sleeping bags, and clothing. And we hit the road.

Max couldn't drive because of a medical condition, so I was the one behind the wheel for the whole trip. Even jam-packed, the old bug was a light car, and the ride was bouncy. As I recollect, we did around three hundred miles a day, which meant at least one fuel-up, usually late in the afternoon. We'd come to a town after crossing a long stretch of desert or climbing over the mountains. Exhausted from driving, I would want to pull in at the first gas station on my right. However, if Max saw one on the left advertising gas for two cents less per gallon, she would demand that I make a U-turn or go around the block. We were sharing expenses, and she insisted that stopping at the closer gas station would be wasting her money. Since the tank held 10.6 gallons, filling it at the first station might have cost her a whole additional twenty cents. I suspected it was a matter of wanting to exert control rather than economic necessity.

We usually camped out in parks or forested areas. Whenever we passed through a flyspeck town or a reservation with a one-room exhibit of local Native American art, Max asked for permission to take pictures of the basketry, weavings, pottery, or anything else usually made by the women.

Then we came to Denver and its art museum. Room after room of display cases, each featuring the work of a particular tribe, and on the wall a plaque with descriptive information about the objects. At the bottom of each plaque were two numbers: the estimated population of the tribe before the Whites came, and how many people in the tribe were left afterward. Just numbers—no narrative of the wars of extermination, the stolen lands, the smallpox-infested blankets.

It was a record of genocide.

I had been feeling sorry for myself, for the demise of my revolutionary dreams and the Women's Press Collective, but my losses were nothing in the face of that horror—or the horrors that my own people had suffered in the Inquisition, through pogrom after pogrom, and most recently, in the Holocaust. The self-pity drained away. Clearly I needed to read some history, to get some perspective. But that would have to wait until we returned to California, and we weren't even halfway to the East Coast yet.

41

MISOGYNY AND HOSPITALITY

AFTER DENVER, MAX AND I headed toward South Dakota, reaching the Badlands late one afternoon, and stopped for a walk. The ground beneath our feet was clay, smooth and slippery, which I found delightful. I could almost skate on it, I thought, or make pots. Pottery wasn't, in fact, a local tradition, I learned—the Native Americans of the area had been nomads and carried everything in baskets, which are much lighter to transport.

It started to rain. That sunset was the most spectacular I've ever seen, with streaks of red clouds in the west, a double rainbow bridging thick charcoal-colored clouds in the east, and lightning dancing across the eastern half of the sky. Back on the road, we drove into darkness and torrential rain. Camping would be impossible. We kept going until we came to a small town with a single run-down motel.

The owners were an elderly couple, looking rather run-down themselves. They didn't move from their chairs but handed us the key to a room. Above the bed were religious pictures: Jesus and Mary with halos and hands over sacred hearts. We turned off the light and made love.

In the morning the sun was shining. I had driven over fifteen hundred miles, and it was time for an oil change, so first thing in the morning I went outside and crawled under the car. While I was working, I saw another car drive up and park a few feet away. A middle-aged man emerged and walked into the motel. Once I'd finished, I went back into the lobby with two jugs of used oil in my hands. "Where can I dispose of these?" I asked.

The owners didn't say anything, but the guy who'd just arrived stared at me. "I'll take care of them," he said. "But I thought that was a *man* under the car."

"It was only me," I replied.

The man shook his head and said, again, "I thought that was a *man* under the car." He added, "You never know what's likely to happen. Why just last year, a White man and a Jewish woman came through here, traveling together! And they weren't even married!"

I ran upstairs, not wanting to find out what the locals would think of two lesbians, one of them Jewish. We grabbed our belongings, jumped in the car, and put that town behind us.

On a hot afternoon somewhere in the Midwest, the bug stopped and wouldn't start again. I steered over to the shoulder. Just as I was lifting the rear deck lid, another car pulled up behind me. Two young men got out and offered to help. "Thanks," I said, "but I'm pretty sure it's vapor lock." I dug a shop rag out of the trunk, wrapped it around the carburetor, and poured cold water on it. After a couple of minutes, I turned the key and the car started again. My would-be saviors did not look happy.

I don't remember all the parks we slept in, except for one in Minnesota. Whoever said the mosquito is their state bird wasn't kidding. Despite the heat, we zipped ourselves up in the sleeping bags, exposing nothing but our nostrils and the hair on top of our heads.

Our next stop was Max's hometown. It grew up around a railroad junction about thirty-five miles west of Chicago and was originally called Turner's Junction, after the president of the railroad. In 1896 the business leaders changed its name to the more cosmopolitan West Chicago, hoping to attract industry. While Max was growing up, the population increased from around thirty-nine hundred to sixty-eight hundred.

We stayed with her mother, who was kind and hospitable, but I was bored by the small talk and didn't know what to say to her, so I spent quite a bit of time working on a thousand-piece jigsaw puzzle. Max was displeased, reasonably enough. The next day she took me on a tour of the town, sharing memories of her childhood.

In Chicago proper we spent the night on a sofa bed in my Aunt Charlotte's apartment. She and her husband (also named Max) were hospitable as well. My Max was already asleep, and I pretended to be, when Charlotte tiptoed in and gazed at us for a while. I wondered what she was thinking.

Eventually we came to Washington, DC, where Max planned to take pictures of exhibits in the Smithsonian. I wasn't familiar with DC, having been there only for antiwar protests, and was pretty sure there wouldn't be a place to camp. Then I thought of my mother's Uncle Ben, who had moved to Silver Spring, Maryland, after his wife died. Would he remember me and let us stay with him?

I dialed the number.

42

BADLY BEHAVED
HOUSE GUESTS

When I told Uncle Ben I was in the area, he said, "Come right over! You know how to get here?"

We bought a map at a gas station and arrived just after dark.

Uncle Ben Bojankosky—my parents always called him the Uncle, because he was the only surviving relative of that generation—was a large, warmhearted guy, balding on top, with soft blue eyes and a Yiddish accent that had hardly diminished over the years. I always admired his courage. He and his brother, my grandfather, were originally from Nowy Dwor, Poland, and they were both in the kosher meat business. After World War I they moved to Havana and then, during the Great Depression, entered the United States without papers. Grandpa was caught and deported to Cuba—and didn't try again. Ben tried a total of four times, was deported three times, and on the fourth attempt, he succeeded in remaining in the United States.

Living in New York, he worked in a sausage factory and saved money to start his own kosher meat dealership. He went bankrupt three times and had to return to the factory. But as with his immigration attempts, on the fourth try he succeeded in the business and was able to retire in relative comfort.

Now he had a one-bedroom condo in a middle-class neighborhood. The building was nice enough and the apartment clean, though sparsely furnished. No doubt his late wife would have hung curtains over the window shades and put a convertible sofa in the living room, but Ben seemed indifferent or at a loss when it came to home decor. A large ironing board with a box of matzos sitting on one end dominated the kitchen.

We unloaded the car and unrolled our sleeping bags on the living room floor. "It isn't very comfortable," Ben said apologetically. "Tomorrow I'll take you to my daughter Sarah's place. You'll have your own bedroom."

Mom's cousin Sarah had visited my family once or twice, many years ago. I was sure she wouldn't recognize me, nor I her, if we fell over each other in Macy's lingerie department. "But Uncle, she doesn't know we're coming—you sure it'll be OK?"

Ben drew back a little, his frown a mix of pride and puzzlement. "Of course," he said. "You're a relative!"

In the morning Ben instructed us to follow his car—a late-model Cadillac. He always had to own a Cadillac, he told me. Perhaps it was to impress customers, or perhaps it was to make up for the poverty of his childhood.

We parked in front of an enormous house in Chevy Chase, Maryland. Ben's daughter had married up. Her husband, Sidney Brown, had a law degree but made his fortune in real estate development and management. As we were walking toward Sarah's front door, Ben told me there had been a recent tragedy in the family: their twenty-four-year-old daughter had committed suicide. I asked why. Ben said Susan had been living with a roommate that her parents disapproved of, and shortly after the parents forced the two girls to separate, Susan overdosed on sleeping pills. It seemed obvious to me what the problem had been, but I didn't inquire further, not wanting to probe an open wound, and also because Ben was already ringing the bell.

Sarah's welcome was pleasant though not enthusiastic—understandable, given the circumstances. She looked a bit like my mother, around five foot two and average weight, but blonder than Mom or her sisters. Max and I were shown to our room, told we could use the swimming pool, and invited to join the family for dinner.

We spent the day at the Smithsonian, as planned, while Max took photos. Then we drove back to the mansion to dine with Sarah and Sidney and their son Stuart, home from college. I remember Sidney being not much taller than his wife. He was a bit on the pudgy side from lack of exercise and wore Coke-bottle glasses. Stuart, maybe twenty or twenty-one, was quite handsome. The dining room, as large as Ben's entire apartment, had high ceilings and Balinese art adorning the walls. An elderly Black maid waited on us.

Max complimented the family on the Balinese paintings. Sarah said they'd been purchased during a trip to Indonesia. "But those people have no culture," she said flatly. "They're primitive."

"What do you mean, no culture?" Max looked up at the artwork again.

Sarah replied that, among other things, they didn't have flush toilets. "Black people have no culture either," she added, right in front of the woman who'd been serving our food.

Max and I were horrified. We couldn't let that pass and began to argue. Then Stuart spoke up. "I think Max has a point."

Sidney rose to his feet and bellowed at his son. "Is *this* what I pay the university to teach you?" The discussion ended there.

The following morning Sarah informed me that she and her husband would be away much of the day, inspecting their properties. After they left, I looked around a bit. Well, I snooped, actually. Lining the hallway were shelves filled with thick leather-bound books, all legal tomes except for a paperback tucked between them that confirmed my suspicions about the daughter: *Lesbian/Woman* by Del Martin and Phyllis Lyon.

Max and I checked out the master bedroom. A king-size bed. On one side, a closet the entire length of the room filled with men's suits. On the other side, a similar closet filled with fur coats. I couldn't imagine what anyone would want with that many furs. Not even a movie star could need such an extravagant collection. Max and I selected one— mink, I suppose—spread it across the bed and made love. Then we hung it back in place.

It was a lovely summer day. We grabbed our swimsuits and went down to the pool. The maid, Mrs. Johnson, was standing under an awning in an alcove beside the pool, doing the ironing. I tried to apologize for Sarah's remarks the previous evening, saying I hoped she didn't think the whole family was like that. She smiled and said it was OK.

A young Black girl sat nearby, looking bored. She introduced herself as Bernice, Mrs. Johnson's granddaughter. "Why don't you join us?" I asked.

"Miz Brown says I can't," Bernice replied, "'cause they don't have a lifeguard."

"I've got a lifeguard certificate," I lied. "If anything happens, I'll save you."

Bernice put on her suit and jumped in. It turned out that she was on the swim team in her high school and was as fast and graceful as a dolphin. "You're much better than I am!" I exclaimed. "You could save *me*." Bernice grinned.

We had been in the water for about an hour when we heard the Browns' car pull up in the driveway. The three of us leaped out of the pool, ran inside, and were back in our street clothes before our hosts could discover us.

Ben came by to check on Max and me that afternoon. After he had chatted with us for a bit, he went to the kitchen and spent some time talking to Mrs. Johnson in his thick Yiddish accent, while she responded in her Southern Black dialect. Sarah, in the next room, obviously disapproved of her father's associations. "I don't know why he talks to her," Sarah said. "They can't possibly understand each other."

Sarah sat on the couch, chain-smoking, and told me how terrible the year had been—first her daughter's suicide and then her own diagnosis with breast cancer. She was obviously in pain and wanted my sympathy. I said something about being sorry, but I was too young and self-righteous to drum up much compassion for her.

Next morning it was time to leave—and at fifteen hundred miles from South Dakota, time for another oil change. I was just tightening the drain plug when Ben arrived, so I scrambled up from under the car to greet him. He smiled and nodded approvingly. "You're just like a Jew from the old country," he said. "Not afraid to get your hands dirty." He directed a significant look at the Brown mansion.

We packed the bug again, said goodbye to the Uncle, and left.

We made two more visits, to my father and sister in New Jersey and to Marge Piercy on Cape Cod, and then headed back to California.

When I told my father about the visit to the Brown mansion (omitting the episode with the mink coat), he wasn't surprised. "I knew Sidney when he was just a small-time slumlord," Dad said with a disgusted look. Later I learned that Sidney Brown had become one of the most notorious slumlords in Washington, DC.

43

IN EXILE

SOON AFTER MAX AND I returned to the Bay Area from our trek across the United States, she proposed that we move to the country for a year. She wanted to continue her research into women's history and write up the information she had gathered on our trip, without the distractions of big-city life.

I was in favor of this plan. I too wanted to do some focused reading and work on my writing. Since the Women's Press Collective had broken up, I had no commitments in Oakland—friends, yes, but no group or project that would tie me there. Seeing the record of genocide against Native Americans at the Denver Art Museum had put my troubles in perspective and given me the impetus to learn more about the history of my own people.

We conducted an exploratory excursion, driving north on I-5 to Mt. Shasta City. Housing there was scarce and pricey. From there we made a loop, going north again past Weed to Yreka and then southwest onto California Highway 3, a two-lane road through little towns, forests, and farm country, up and down over the hills between the Shasta and Scott Valleys. We finally found a rental in Etna, population around 730.

Or rather, Max did. She secured a garden apartment attached to a large house at the south end of town. She didn't want to share space with me, perhaps because she preferred living alone at that time in her life, or because she'd had enough of me after our cross-country road trip, or possibly because she didn't want our relationship to be obvious in that conservative town. In any case, she took the apartment for herself and left me to find my own place. What if all I could find was in another town, even as far as Mt. Shasta, sixty miles away? She didn't seem to care. I was hurt, but said nothing. Fortunately, the Etna Hotel, which was right in the center of town, had a vacancy.

The hotel was a two-story building on Main Street, tucked between stores and offices, and had probably seen better days. My suite—I suppose you could call it that—was on the second floor. It had a small kitchen and a combination bedroom/living room with comfortable but well-worn furniture. The sweet elderly couple who owned the place lived downstairs. They were country people, the man mainly interested in hunting and fishing, the woman obsessed with making pies. I was lucky enough to taste one of her delicious creations.

Max's landlady was far from being sweet. After Max had planted a few vegetables in the backyard, Mrs. Tomkiewicz put her horse there, and it devoured the greens and carpeted the yard with manure. Later, Mrs. T. removed the beast and told Max she could start over if she wanted to.

Aside from the Etna Hotel, the little town featured a small convenience store, a soda shop, a one-room bookstore, a hardware store, a one-room library, and five churches.

Max didn't seem interested in the community or the locals. She had grown up in a small town. I had lived only in New York City and the San Francisco Bay Area, so this was a new world for me, and I reached out, exploring and making friends.

I discovered on my first visit that the woman who staffed the one-room library was a John Bircher and stocked their propaganda, so I never entered the place again. Dorothy, who owned the bookstore, was more congenial. I browsed through her wares and bought some, and we chatted. When I let her know that I was a lesbian, she said that in her younger days she'd had a crush on another woman. It seemed she could have taken that road, but she loved living in the country and was an ardent fisherwoman, so I suppose she chose a path that allowed her to fit into the rural life.

Corky, the hardware store owner, had moved from a big city to raise children in what he considered a healthy environment. He was earnest and honest and a member of the Scott Valley Berean Church. I bought automotive oil and other supplies from him. Over a quarter century later, when I visited Etna again, he recognized me and called me by name.

In addition to the Berean church, a fundamentalist Christian denomination, Etna also had a Methodist church, a Mormon church, a Catholic church, and a Russian Orthodox monastery. Max and I attended one of the Berean services—only one. Aside from our not being Christian, whatever friendly interest we may have had vanished when the congregation sang: "Trust and obey / for that's the only way / to be happy in Jesus / is to trust and obey." Not a message likely to appeal to anti-capitalist, rebellious lesbian feminists.

I did become friends with Marilyn Seward, the minister's wife. She was highly energetic as well as capable and kind. At one point she told me that if she hadn't been a Christian, she would've become a feminist. She also taught school when I knew her. Later, after we were no longer in Etna, she served on various local corporate boards, and during one period was mayor of the town while continuing to be active in the church. Definitely a woman of action.

I also had conversations with Marilyn's husband, Wendell. When I asked him whether any Jews lived in the area, he said there were some Jews for Jesus. "If they worship Jesus, they're Christians, not Jews," I replied. I didn't ask if there were any other lesbians. However, near the end of our stay—too late for friendship—I did finally encounter a lesbian couple who lived deeper in the woods, in an unincorporated community called Somes Bar, population 203.

One day Max and I read that the local community college was sponsoring a class in Karuk, a local Native American language. We signed up, thinking, somewhat childishly, that we could learn a language hardly anyone else knew—today there are only ten fluent speakers—and use it for secret communication. The teacher was a middle-aged Native woman who, because of an illness in her family, had been kept at home as a child instead of being taken forcibly to boarding school, where she would have been forbidden to speak Karuk. The other students were also middle-aged Native women. Max and I picked up the words fairly easily, but our classmates struggled and finally gave up, and the class disbanded. For years I felt guilty about it, thinking that we had discouraged the Native women, until my wife, Sylvia, pointed out that many people lack the ability to learn a new language as adults.

During our year in Etna, Max and I developed routines. Most days we read, wrote, and hiked, or sometimes went backpacking. Etna is located at the foot of the Marble Mountain Wilderness. There was a deep pool right at the closest trailhead. In summer we would dive off a huge boulder into the water, and once we had cooled off, we'd hoist our packs and head in. One of my favorite memories of our time in Etna is of a winter hike. We trudged uphill until we were pouring sweat, then stripped naked and rolled in the snow.

On Saturdays we drove the thirty miles over the hill to Yreka, shopped at the supermarket, took out books from the local Siskiyou County Library, and ate at a Mexican restaurant. The library was a treasure. Between the collections on their shelves and interlibrary loans, I was able to delve into Jewish history and, in addition, learn more about the local history and natural sciences. A book I liked well enough to purchase later was *In the Land of the Grasshopper Song*. It recounts the first-person experiences of two White women who in 1908 were recruited by the United States Indian Service to travel from their home in Brooklyn and spend two years among the Karuk Indians in the Klamath River area.

The women, Mary Ellicott Arnold and Mabel Reed, were assigned to educate and assimilate. Once there, however, they decided that the Karuks were doing fine on their own and did not need assimilation. They focused instead on teaching math and English. Among those they befriended was a Native woman, Essie, who had three husbands. Far from attempting to dissuade Essie from this polyandrous arrangement, Mary and Mabel approved. Essie could count on three men to do the heavy work, and she would often send them to Mary and Mabel, who had the benefit of their services "with no embarrassment and none of the problems."

What first aroused my suspicions, though, was the description of their stay at a dingy hotel in Weitchpec, on the way to the Karuk village. "That night in the sagging bed we clutched each other and tried to keep warm." And wherever they went, throughout the book, they shared a bed. According to the publisher of a reprint, they had met as children and "were an adventurous and devoted twosome for nearly seventy years."

Every two or three months we would drive down to the Bay Area to visit people and luxuriate in a lesbian-friendly environment. Arriving there felt like loosening the stays of a corset. At the end of the year Max and I moved back to Oakland and found new apartments—again, separately. Shortly thereafter we broke up.

DISCOVERING JEZEBEL

About halfway through that year in Etna, reading the Bible as a way to learn about my people, about their way of understanding their history and struggles, I found a passage that would once again change the course of my life. In the two Books of Kings, I discovered Jezebel. I had always known her name as an epithet for a sexually immoral woman. But reading the text, I quickly realized that that made no sense. Such misbehavior on Jezebel's part isn't even suggested in the biblical account, which was written by her enemies. How could the wife of an Israelite king get away with sexual promiscuity, anyway? Her every move was known. She would have been killed. And did Jezebel really arrange the murder of Navot so that her husband, Ahab, could take over his vineyard? Or, as has happened in so many situations, was the woman blamed for the man's misdeeds?

I determined to restore Jezebel's reputation in the form of a novel. First, though, I had a lot to learn. Most novels based on stories in the Bible are intended to inspire belief rather than question it. If I disputed the traditional version of Jezebel, I wouldn't be taken seriously unless I backed up my tale with historical evidence. When we returned to the Bay Area, I began to scour scholarly journals and books about life in the ancient Middle East and to study Hebrew. I traveled to Israel and the West Bank and spent some months visiting archeological sites and museum exhibits.

That research, which I thought might take another year at most, would become central to my life and take me on many unexpected journeys. Along with teaching myself to write fiction, I co-parented five children, took a master's degree in teaching English as a second language, published three more books of poetry, and started a business. Those adventures, however, are another story. The Jezebel novel grew into a trilogy. Now the work is completed and is in print. You can find it at www.ebisupublications.com.

———————

Interviewers often ask me what advice I have for young activists today. The short answer is, they don't need our advice. They don't need it any more than we needed the advice of our elders. Like us, they need to know the history. They need to know what worked and what didn't. But conditions change. If we had done what the older activists told us to, we'd still be back where we were, trying to make nice with people who just wanted to crush us, or make us disappear.

However, if young activists did ask my advice, I'd say three things: first, make connections with people in other social justice movements. Find out what they need, how you can help, and make alliances. The second thing is, we have to keep fighting! Even if we have won some rights, in each generation someone will be trying to take them away. That's happening today. It's been happening in the United States since the 1980s, when Reagan began his assault on unions, pushing back on every gain workers made during the New Deal. Now the would-be fascists intend to wipe out the advances of the 1960s and '70s, and more.

Still, if we lose ground and they're coming down hard on us, keep fighting anyway! There will be setbacks. Victories don't happen overnight, but they won't happen at all if we give up. Rabbi Tarfon said, "You are not obligated to complete the work, but neither are you free to abandon it." The job of an activist is never done.

Finally, not only don't ask your elders for advice, but don't wait for a leader to tell you what to do either. Don't wait for the politicians who take money from your enemies. You are the leader. You are the one who can make the change. Every one of you.

ACKNOWLEDGMENTS

To my wife, Sylvia Allen, goes my utmost gratitude. Without her encouragement and editing of each chapter as I produced them, this work would not exist.

I am also immensely grateful to Barbara Joans, for listening while I read chapters aloud and for tales of her experiences and exploits in the women's movement, some of which are incorporated here.

Equal gratitude and heartfelt salutes go to Phyllis Chesler and to Fern Sidman for their encouragement throughout, their insistence on the importance of this story, and their conviction that my efforts will meet with success. Phyllis also deserves special honors for referring me to the publisher.

Two big shout-outs go to Nadine Fiedler and Seiza de Tarr for reading the manuscript and for their suggestions.

I send many thanks and virtual hugs to my sister, Jeannette Hoffman; my brother, Ira Terman; and cousins Lorraine Fox and Larry Kleinman for sharing their memories.

And last, only because his contribution is the most recent, I have been greatly honored to work with Jerome Pohlen and Devon Freeny of Chicago Review Press. They have my deepest appreciation for their efforts in turning the manuscript into an actual, real-life book.

NOTES

1. A Small Act of Rebellion

"really dangerous Communist would": Editorial opposing the New York State's Feinberg Law, *New York Times*, December 4, 1950. Among other things, the law required the state to draw up a list of "subversive" organizations and fire any teacher who had ever belonged to one. It also required a loyalty oath from all public employees. The *Times* supported the oath but not the other provisions.

2. Origins

"During the war the government": Robert Higgs, "Wartime Prosperity? A Reassessment of the U.S. Economy in the 1940s," *The Independent Institute*, March 1, 1992, reprinted from *The Journal of Economic History* 52, no. 1 (March 1992), published by Cambridge University Press.

11. A Cult in the City

"Most members lived in": Jake Offenhartz, "Inside the Rise and Fall of a 1970s Upper West Side Cult," *Gothamist*, September 21, 2016.

17. The Night We Set on Fire

"Heavy police reinforcements cleared": "Police Again Rout 'Village Youths,'" *New York Times*, June 30, 1969. This is an initial account of the Stonewall Riots. There had been previous resistance to police raids, in Los Angeles and in San Francisco, but nothing much came of them. What made Stonewall different—and historic—was that we organized the Gay Liberation Front almost immediately afterward. Subsequently, GLF groups sprang up around the nation and in the UK and Canada. Together with offshoots like Gay Activists Alliance, Radicalesbians, Street Transvestite Action Revolutionaries (STAR), Third World Gay Revolutionaries, Parents and Friends of Lesbians and Gays (PFLAG), we were able to make vast social changes.

19. *WE* Are the Gay Liberation Front!

including one I wrote: Martha Shelley, "Stepin Fetchit Woman," *Come Out!* (New York) 1, no. 1 (November 14, 1969): 7.

21. Fighting on All Fronts

"the slim-waisted creeps": Howard Kurtz, "A Straight and Narrow Path," *Washington Post*, June 3, 1996. The article recounts some of the vicious slurs directed against gays by the media.

22. *RAT* Newspaper—and Some Real Rats

An article I wrote: Martha Shelley, "Gay Is Good," most recently reprinted in *The Movements of the New Left, 1950–1975*, ed. V. Gosse (New York: Palgrave Macmillan, 2005), 137–141.

23. Occupying the Porn Factory

"Grove Press won't let women": David M. Dismore, "Today in Feminist History: Women Stage Sit-in at NYC's Grove Press (April 13, 1970)," MSmagazine.com, April 13, 2020, https://msmagazine.com/2020/04/13/today-in-feminist-history -women-stage-sit-in-at-nycs-grove-press-april-13-1970/.

24. A Menace Grabs the Mic

the speakers at the rally included: Linda Charlton, "Women March Down Fifth in Equality Drive," *New York Times*, August 27, 1970.

35. Martha Got Her Guns

"I killed the son of a bitch": Lousie Bernikow, "1974 Rape Trial Spurred Women's Quest for Justice," *Women's eNews*, September 30, 2008, https://womens enews.org/2008/09/1974-rape-trial-spurred-womens-quest-justice/.

"The gun control advocacy group": Moira Donegan, "The American Gun Crisis? It's Largely a Domestic Violence Crisis," *Guardian*, May 13, 2021.

36. In Print and on the Road

"It's funny that in 1976": Frances Doughty, "Charlotte Bunch on Women's Publishing," *Sinister Wisdom* 13 (Spring 1980).

38. A Dream Comes Undone

I was recently forwarded: Carol Shull, "They're Reducing the Cost and the Trauma of Abortions," *Argus* (Fremont, CA), May 10, 1973.

At the end of the year: "Abortions, Legal for Year, Performed for Thousands," *New York Times*, December 31, 1973.

43. In Exile

"with no embarrassment": Mary Ellicott Arnold and Mabel Reed, *In the Land of the Grasshopper Song* (New York: Vantage Press, 1957), 68.

"That night in the sagging bed": Arnold and Reed, 27.

"were an adventurous and devoted twosome": Mary Ellicott Arnold and Mabel Reed, *In the Land of the Grasshopper Song* (1957; repr., Lincoln, NE: University of Nebraska Press, 1980), back cover copy.